THE MAKING OF A WOMAN

She was only 14 when she first met Elvis Presley and fell under his spell.... But it was five years before Elvis declared her fit to be his bride, after he had obsessively schooled her in everything from how to please his eyes to how to please his senses.... Her marriage was a mingling of glorious fulfillment and growing fear, glamour and heartbreak, as she helplessly watched the tender, giving man she loved moving away from her on a path of self-destruction.... Her divorce was the end of everything, until it turned into the beginning of a career that would take her to a starring role in *Dallas* and coast-to-coast fame on her own....

This is the one book that tells it all—the good times and the bad, the laughter and the tears, and the triumph over all the odds against a woman who had to learn to live and love all over again....

PRISCILLA AND ELVIS
The Priscilla Presley Story

PRISCILLA ☆ AND ☆ ELVIS

The Priscilla Presley Story

by

Caroline Latham

WITH 8 PAGES OF PHOTOS

A SIGNET BOOK

NEW AMERICAN LIBRARY

Copyright © 1985 by Caroline Latham

Photos courtesy of AP/Wide World Photos.

SIGNET TRADEMARK REG. U.S. PAT. OFF. AND FOREIGN COUNTRIES
REGISTERED TRADEMARK—MARCA REGISTRADA
HECHO EN CHICAGO, U.S.A.

SIGNET, SIGNET CLASSIC, MENTOR, PLUME, MERIDIAN
and NAL BOOKS are published by New American Library,
1633 Broadway, New York, New York 10019

First Printing, December, 1985

1 2 3 4 5 6 7 8 9

PRINTED IN THE UNITED STATES OF AMERICA

Contents

Chapter 1

☆ ☆ ☆

A Love Story
for Our Times

Priscilla Beaulieu Presley has lived one of the strangest, yet most romantic, love stories of our time.

When Priscilla was only 14 years old, a schoolgirl living at home with her parents and five brothers and sisters, she met Elvis Presley. The year was 1959. Elvis was already the idol of millions, the King of rock and roll, one of the best-known faces and voices in the entire world. To Priscilla's enormous surprise Elvis showed unmistakable signs of interest in her. A few years later, while she was still in high school, Priscilla went to live at Graceland with Elvis. She grew up under his watchful eye; Elvis Presley was her finishing school. Most of his friends and family agreed that he was in the process of molding her into the woman of his dreams.

Elvis's dreams—and Priscilla's, too—seemed to come true a few years later when they were married in a ceremony that appropriately took place in a Las Vegas hotel.

Exactly nine months later they became the parents of a baby girl. Yet the dream proved to be short-lived. Three years after the baby was born the couple separated. The following year, 1973, they were divorced.

Interestingly, there were signs that not even divorce could put an end to the romance between Elvis and Priscilla. They were photographed emerging from the divorce court holding hands, and Elvis kissed her tenderly and whispered words of love in her ear as they parted. Each found other partners, but people close to both of them always half expected to hear that they were getting back together again. That possibility was ended when Elvis died on August 16, 1977.

The story of Elvis and Priscilla is both highly unusual and completely familiar. Few women meet their future husbands at the age of 14 and live with them for the formative years of their teens. Even fewer marry rich and famous men who can literally give them anything they want. And only one could marry Elvis Presley, with his curious combination of enormous talent, great animal magnetism, even greater childishness of behavior, and serious emotional problems that eventually caused the tragedy of his death at 42.

But if you look past the parts of the story that could have happened only to Priscilla and Elvis, you see the outlines of a story that is typical of many couples. A romance develops between a man who is older and more successful and a younger woman who has not yet had the time to accomplish much on her own but has obvious potential. She loves and admires him for his ability to deal with the world so smoothly, his knowledge of things she is only just learning, his stature in the eyes of others. He loves her because she admires his intelligence, because she doesn't criticize him, because she makes him feel more skilled or more successful than he secretly believes himself to be.

But then time passes and things change. The woman grows older, learns more, realizes that she wants to use her potential to achieve on her own. She no longer desires a mentor but an equal; she no longer believes that everything he says or does is automatically right. Her new point of view comes as an unpleasant surprise to him and seems to rob him of the things he sought in the relationship. He expected always to be the senior partner, and suddenly he finds that he can't even count on being first among equals. Both parties are badly disillusioned, and commonly the relationship is ended.

This is the Elvis and Priscilla Presley story. Priscilla made the marriage that many women dream of. Her husband was older, richer, more successful, more prominent. He had the wealth to shower her with an endless stream of gifts, and he had the power to create a private world in which she could live, eternally cherished as his wife and the mother of his child. What's more, he genuinely loved her, and he was an extremely romantic soul. Before he and Priscilla were married, he confessed to columnist May Mann, "When I marry, it will be a very sure thing—to be forever, like my Mama and my Daddy. I'll have a big church wedding, do it proper, with flowers and music and the whole thing. . . . When I see a girl as sweet as my Mama, and as beautiful, I could get marriage-minded right away—if the real love is there."

Once they were married, everyone agreed that Elvis put Priscilla on a pedestal. She was not to work and not to worry. She had an unlimited checking account and was surrounded by an entourage ready to satisfy her slightest whim. A new fur coat? A trip to Las Vegas for the weekend? A new house to decorate as she pleased? All she had to do was ask.

What neither Elvis nor Priscilla had foreseen was that she would become dissatisfied with this dream world. She wanted to be her own person, have her own successes, make her own choices. Inside her dream world she was slowly strangling. She understood that it was a problem she shared with many other women, seemingly the lucky ones with lovely homes and generous husbands. "They aren't doing what they really want to do," she comments. "So many women don't because they're scared to. And they don't do what they were meant to do: flourish." Priscilla was brave enough to decide to try to change her life. She left Elvis and struck out on her own. There were years of emotional struggle and pain, but eventually she began to reap the rewards. "I became confident, in control of my life, secure: all the things I couldn't be before."

Her departure was a grave emotional blow to Elvis. He, too, went through a great deal of pain, and some people feel that he never got over it. There are those who still blame Priscilla for that decision; she is the wife who walked out on him, and they'll never forgive her. But Priscilla herself knows the inner truth of their relationship. She has revealed that after their divorce Elvis eventually came to the realization that she had been right in seeking the chance to stand on her own two feet and take charge of her own life. She talks about a telephone conversation they had, not too long before he died. "We had the most beautiful talks, the closest moments, at the very end. He'd say, 'Cilla, you were right. I *should* have given you more freedom. I should have listened when you said you needed to have your own friends over to the house. I know why I didn't let you: It was my own insecurity.'" He cheered her on as she struggled to achieve genuine independence and finally gave her the one thing she most wanted from him: respect.

The love story of Elvis and Priscilla is a touching and sentimental one. It also has its dark side, which mirrored Elvis's own problems and insecurities—the drug use, the womanizing, the tensions that were the result of his secret definition of sex as shameful, the inability to grow up and leave the security of his gang of yes-men. It is at once typical of many romances and absolutely unique. Most of all, it has a fascinating quality of being larger than life: more love, more pain, more drama than most of us experience in a lifetime.

Priscilla Beaulieu Presley is today a successful actress, a good and caring mother, a fascinating person. She has achieved what she set out to do: She has become a person in her own right, and an interesting and admirable one at that. Above all, she has found the strength of the survivor. She is the woman who lived the love story of Elvis and Priscilla.

Chapter 2

☆ ☆ ☆

Meeting Elvis

Priscilla was a 14-year-old schoolgirl when she met Elvis Presley, who was already a world-famous idol.

In many ways she was just an ordinary girl. She loved animals and worried about being popular. She was a Girl Scout who had to set the table for dinner every night and help do the dishes afterward. She fantasized about kissing boys but avoided situations where the fantasy might turn into reality. Like most other teenage girls in the late 1950s, she was a fan of Elvis Presley. But he wasn't her only favorite. She also liked to hear Frankie Avalon singing "Venus" and the Everly Brothers with "All I Have to Do Is Dream."

Priscilla's family seemed All-American too. Her mother was an ex-model, a pretty woman who had made her family the center of her life. Her father was a career Air Force officer, so the family moved frequently. Priscilla had lived in New York, Connecticut, and Texas, before her father was stationed in Wiesbaden, Germany. Priscilla remembers that he was "a very strict father who would say no without having to give you a reason." The family was run with a sense of military discipline. Rules were rules; children did as they were told. Priscilla was the oldest of six children in the family. She had one younger sister and four brothers, including a set of twins. A responsible big sister, she helped her mother look after the younger children.

Though the early years of her life seemed quite ordinary, the young Priscilla possessed an unusual spirit. She was an extremely romantic girl, and given to fantastic daydreams. One of the objects of her fantasies was the singer Mario Lanza. "From the time I was nine I had an affinity for him. I loved his music and I had been told he was very lonely and I identified with that. I used to play his records and talk to him and try to make him feel better." Her sense of loneliness seemed to run deep. Moving frequently may have had something to do with it. "It makes you grow up with a very insecure feeling," she recalls. "You begin to wonder who your friends are—and what *are* friends."

Perhaps another source of her lonely feelings was her discovery of the fact that Paul Beaulieu was not her real father. Her mother had been married before, to a Navy pilot, Lieutenant James Wagner. He was killed in a crash when Priscilla was just six months

old. Several years later Priscilla's mother re-
married, and her new husband adopted her
daughter. Priscilla was happy and secure
with her family, but she carried within her
some sense that she was different.

Priscilla says that her dreams when she
was small could best be described by seeing
The Black Stallion; she saw herself as lonely
but special, on her own but self-sufficient.
"I always knew that something extraordinary was going to happen to me," she told
a reporter.

The extraordinary event began when the
Beaulieu family moved to Wiesbaden. Priscilla had hated to leave Austin, even after
one of her girlfriends tried to comfort her
by pointing out that Elvis Presley was also
stationed in Germany in that year of 1959.
They looked it up on a map; he was in Bad
Nauheim, only a few miles away from Wiesbaden. The joke that she was "going to Germany to meet Elvis Presley" cheered Priscilla
up at a depressing moment in her young
life.

In Germany she felt even lonelier and more
isolated. The one place, outside of home,
that seemed welcoming was the snack bar
at the Eagles Club, a hangout for American
military families. She often stopped in after
school to have a Coke and play the jukebox.
One day she was approached there by an
older man in an Air Force uniform. He asked
her if she liked Elvis Presley, and, of course,

she said yes. Then he asked her if she'd like to meet him.

Priscilla was a well-brought-up girl, and she was immediately suspicious of this seemingly outlandish invitation. But her father checked out the airman, named Currie Grant, and his story was true. He and his wife had become friendly with Elvis, and Elvis liked to surround himself with people, especially Americans, who helped to alleviate his own homesickness. The Grants often brought guests to the house Elvis rented off-base in Bad Nauheim for what amounted to a nightly party. Elvis played records and occasionally sang, himself. Soft drinks and snacks (Elvis's favorite was a few pounds of bacon fried up crisp) were served by his grandmother. It seemed an innocent enough way to spend an evening. The Beaulieus decided that their daughter should have her chance to meet the famous Elvis Presley. She'd have that special memory all the rest of her life.

Priscilla remembers how carefully she dressed for that wonderful occasion. She tried on a number of different outfits but ended up in a white sailor dress with white shoes and socks. It did nothing to make her look older or more sophisticated, but she thought she succeeded in looking "cute." According to Elvis's stepmother, Dee Presley (then dating Vernon Presley but not yet married to him), Priscilla was right. "She was as cute as a petite Dresden doll. Her hair was one long brown mane of curls that hung down her shoulder, and she had a little button nose. She was a very well-mannered girl, very sophisticated for her age, but not pretentious."

Priscilla, in a 1979 interview, told a reporter about the exact moment of meeting. "I walked in the door and there—sitting across the room in a red sweater—was Elvis. I went over in my little sailor dress and said hello. I felt so... *young*." In that moment Priscilla Beaulieu caught Elvis's eye. Years later Priscilla told Elvis's secretary, Becky Yancey, more details about that first meeting. "Elvis was just wonderful. He sang and played the piano. He was very charming. Would you believe it, he got up and shook my hand when I walked in and said, 'Hi, I'm Elvis Presley.'" Elvis was surprised when she told him that she was only in the ninth grade but nevertheless unmistakably attracted. In her own book, *Elvis and Me,* Priscilla recalled, "I glanced up and saw Elvis trying to get my attention. I noticed that the less response I showed, the more he began singing just for me. I couldn't believe that Elvis Presley was trying to impress me."

All in all, it was an evening that exceeded all her fantasy expectations. The famous Elvis Presley seemed warm and friendly, easy to talk to, interested in hearing about what the kids back home in Texas were listening to on the radio. To the 14-year-old Priscilla the meeting must have seemed like a magic moment that would live forever in her memory, something she would eventually take pleasure in telling her grandchildren: "Tell us again, Gramma, about the time you met Elvis Presley."

The evening ended with an abrupt crash back to reality. She stayed a little longer than she should have, and there was a heavy fog that night, forcing Currie Grant to creep along the Autobahn on the way back to Wiesbaden. It was nearly two A.M. when Priscilla got home, much to her parents' annoyance. "They were waiting up for us when Currie got me home, and Dad was mad. I told him there was nothing wrong, that three or four of Elvis's friends were there with their dates and a couple of other girls. It was all so very informal and natural." Captain Beaulieu was not particularly reassured by his daughter's words, and he told Priscilla flatly that she couldn't go to Elvis's house again.

She assumed that it was an academic argument. She'd had her glimpse of the famous Elvis Presley, and even though she thought he'd noticed her, she didn't expect to be invited back again. She was, after all, just a kid—and he was a famous star. "I didn't think it made much difference anyway, because I figured that I would never see him again. Then he called, and I couldn't have been more surprised."

Elvis had his heart set on seeing the girl in the sailor suit again. Priscilla talked it over with her mother, who saw how much it meant to her daughter, and finally agreed to intercede with her father and ask for his permission to go back one more time. Ann Beaulieu didn't even like Elvis Presley, but it seemed reasonable that her daughter wanted to take advantage of this opportunity to see the teenage idol one more time. At that point it obviously hadn't occurred to Ann that Elvis Presley might be personally interested in her young daughter. She just saw it as a lucky chance to meet a real celebrity... it might give her shy, lonely daughter a bit of self-confidence to be able to tell the other girls at school that she had met Elvis. Faced with this double-barreled pleading from his womenfolk, Priscilla's father gave in: "Just this once."

But once stretched on. There was another time, and another, and finally the Beaulieus had to face the facts. Their daughter, Priscilla, who hadn't yet had a real date since she was only in the ninth grade, was "keeping company" with Elvis Presley. It must have been a bewildering turn of events for her parents. They had just barely begun to worry about the possibility that their daughter would start dating some pimply-faced adolescent who might want to kiss her, when suddenly she was being pursued by the foremost sex symbol of the decade. Like many other mothers, Ann Beaulieu had been complaining, only a few years earlier, about the lewd effect of Elvis's swinging hips, the long hair hanging down over the sultry bedroom eyes, and his pouty, suggestive mouth. Now her daughter was spending long evenings in the man's company.

Faced with a very difficult situation, Priscilla's parents decided to ignore the fact that Elvis Presley was internationally famous and treat him like any other boyfriend—really an impossible task, as they were soon to discover.

Their first step was to decree that before Priscilla could see Elvis again, they would have to meet him. Elvis promptly agreed to this demand, providing that he could bring his father along for moral support. Needless to say, Priscilla was a nervous wreck as she waited for Elvis and Vernon to appear, and she tried to calm herself down by playing one of Elvis's records on the phonograph. Suddenly her father bellowed, "Do you have to play those records now? My God, the man will be here in a few minutes and you see him practically every night. I'd think you'd want to take a breather from each other." Elvis Presley *wasn't* just another date, after all.

Elvis drove up in his BMW. He was wearing his army uniform to impress upon Captain Beaulieu that he, too, was a military man. He walked right in the door, extended his hand, and said, "Hello, I'm Elvis Presley." He called Priscilla's father "sir" or "Captain Beaulieu." Captain Beaulieu was somewhat mollified by this show of respectful manners, but he stuck with his own agenda. He asked Elvis about his intentions toward Priscilla, and Elvis answered that he was "very fond of her" and "enjoyed her company." Then Captain Beaulieu told Elvis that he could continue to see Priscilla on one condition: that he *personally* had to bring her home afterward. Elvis, who liked to rely on the people around him to take care of such mundane chores, agreed. The two men shook hands again on their bargain. Priscilla was amazed by Elvis's tractability, and impressed by the fact that he was willing to go through so much just to have her company.

Their long courtship had begun.

Chapter 3

☆ ☆ ☆

The German Interlude

When Elvis Presley and Priscilla Beaulieu met, they were both very vulnerable people.

Priscilla was vulnerable because she was young and romantic. She was meeting a man she knew to be the idol of millions—who was she to remain unmoved by his obvious interest? She had just moved to a new school, this time in a country where she didn't even speak the language. She had that teenage fear that she wouldn't fit in, that she wouldn't be "popular" in her new environment. She was afraid that the kids at her new school wouldn't like her. Suddenly she had Elvis Presley at her feet. What 14-year-old girl could resist?

But Elvis, too, was feeling vulnerable during that fall of 1959. Since he'd burst on the scene and became an immediate star in the mid-1950s, things had been happening very fast. And then, just the previous summer, his entire world had collapsed when his beloved mother had died. She had been in poor health for some years, and her way of life had made a bad matter worse. A close friend

of the family explained what happened to
Gladys Presley. "She wanted to be what she
thought Elvis wanted her to be. She wanted
to look good for Elvis, to be thin and attractive. But she was not supposed to be
thin, and she stayed heavy, began to put on
more weight. She began to take pills. Diet
pills. I guess they became a habit with her.
And then she switched to alcohol. All she
wanted was to make Elvis proud. She just
wanted him to be proud of her. And, of
course, he *was* proud of her. But she kept
on taking those pills and drinking . . . and
finally her big ol' heart gave out." She'd been
only 46.

It is impossible to tell how much of this
analysis Elvis understood or accepted. Did
he recognize that even though Gladys kept
urging him to get married, she was also
trying to compete with the women he was
attracted to? Did he see the self-destructive
element in her behavior? Did it strike a note
of familiarity? There is no concrete answer
to any of these questions. What we do know
is that his mother's death was a serious
emotional blow to Elvis.

Just a few weeks after the funeral, Elvis's
army unit was sent to West Germany. He told
the press, "One of the last things Mom said
was that Dad and I should always be together. Wherever they send me, Dad will go
too. . . . Mom and Dad and I often talked

about going to Europe. I guess that's where we'll go now—the two of us."

From the very beginning of his stint in the army, Elvis had faced a virtually impossible set of demands. He had to appear to be "one of the guys"; any hint that he wanted special treatment would have done serious damage to his public image and seriously upset his fans (and their parents). Yet, in fact, he couldn't be just another guy in the army, because he couldn't appear in public without virtually starting a riot. He had to be protected, kept away from the eager fans and the even more eager press. A compromise solution to this problem allowed Elvis to live off-base, in much the same way that he used to live at Graceland, just so long as he reported in every morning to do his army duty.

Elvis had never particularly liked to be alone, and now that his mother was gone, he was even more determined to surround himself with familiar faces. There was Vernon, of course, and there was also his grandmother, Minnie Mae Presley, nicknamed Dodger. Lamar Fike was there, all three hundred pounds of him; Lamar had been the first of the entourage that formed when Elvis had become famous. Red West, who had been friends with Elvis in high school, was in Germany for a while. And there were two newcomers to the still forming entourage, Charlie Hodge and Joe Esposito, both servicemen also stationed in Germany. All these men would be Elvis stalwarts for most of his years in the spotlight. They ran interference for Elvis, kept fans away or brought them in, depending on his mood. They dashed out for cheeseburgers and cooked up a few pounds of bacon when Elvis was hungry. They literally watched over him day and night, keeping guard to make sure he didn't walk in his sleep, a childhood habit that made him afraid he would come to harm without even knowing it.

Some or all of these people could always be found in the three-bedroom house Elvis had rented for himself, his daddy, and his grandmother in Bad Nauheim, at 14 Goethestrasse. When Priscilla first started visiting him there, the atmosphere seemed like a perpetual sock hop. At first that seemed like a lot of fun, but then she noticed that it meant she had very little time alone with Elvis. It was his way of keeping the loneliness and the fears at bay, and he was to do it all the rest of his life.

Surrounding himself with people helped Elvis ignore some of those sad feelings, but it didn't make them go away. He felt especially low after his father met Dee Stanley, then married to a career officer stationed in Germany. It was quickly apparent that Vernon's feelings for Dee were serious and that it was just a matter of time before they married. Although Elvis never blamed his father

for taking another wife, he did feel a fresh
sense of abandonment. His mother wanted
the two of them to stay together always, and
now Vernon had already found another person to relieve his loneliness.

So there was Elvis Presley, thousands of
miles from home. He was still grieving for
the loss of his mother and now had to face
a degree of emotional separation from his
father. He was worried about his career,
afraid that two years in the army without a
single performance or appearance would
make even the most devoted fans forget all
about him, replace him in their affections
with some new star. A sincere and patriotic
young man, Elvis was doing his best to fit
into the highly disciplined world of the army.
But there was a clash of values and attitudes
between the army and the life of a famous
rock star, and that put him under a lot of
pressure. In his own house in the evenings,
after he left the army base, he re-created the
environment he had left behind. There was
a sign outside the door that read, AUTO-
GRAPHS BETWEEN 7 AND 8 P.M. *ONLY,* and the
usual entourage inside, keeping Elvis as
happy as possible. He would stay up all
night, listening to records, playing his guitar or the piano and singing, hanging out
with the guys and accepting the admiration
of the girls. Then the next morning he would
get up at the crack of dawn and go out on
maneuvers. This was the time Elvis discov-

ered the magic of Dexedrine, the ampheta-
mine used chiefly to control appetite, which
could make such a balancing act possible.

So perhaps Elvis was as vulnerable as
Priscilla. He needed to feel close to someone
special, and he wanted to feel that he was
loved for himself. Priscilla's youth and in-
nocence appeared to him to be a sort of
guarantee of the purity of her devotion. He
could relax with her, tell her his secrets, trust
her to understand and sympathize. Meanwhile he could teach her to grow up to be
the sort of woman he could really fall in love
with....

Everyone who saw Elvis and Priscilla together in those months in Germany was
struck by his genuine interest in her. Dee
Presley, in the book about Elvis she wrote
with her sons, *Elvis: We Love You Tender,*
said, "When Elvis met her, it was obvious to
Dee that he liked her because he behaved
funny around her, like a high-school kid
trying to impress his date with funny an-
tics. They began seeing more of each other,
riding around in Elvis's BMW and spending
time at the house on Goethestrasse."

Dee remembers Elvis's Christmas party
that year and how attracted to her Elvis
seemed. "The place was filled with very sophisticated women, many of them trying
their best to attract Elvis's eye. Dee and Vernon had gone to pick up Priscilla to bring
her to the party. Cilla was dressed very sim-

ply in a print dress with a high collar," Dee
recalls, "and all of the other women were in
low-cut things. She was the prettiest girl
there, and Elvis couldn't take his eyes off
her the whole night."

Elvis's German secretary, Elisabeth Ste-
faniak, also thought Elvis was different with
Priscilla than he was with the other girls.
"It's like she could get away with more smart
talk than the other girls. He could put them
in their place real quick, but not her." There
was a precocious worldliness about Priscilla
that allowed her to hold her own with the
famous star. And Elvis appreciated another
quality in her, as Dee Presley put it, "a quality he would insist on in his women: class—
plus intelligence, a graceful poise, social
adroitness and a sense of self-awareness."
In a mature woman these qualities might
have struck Elvis as rather threatening. But
in a 14-year-old, they were very appealing.
Years later Elvis told a reporter, "Priscilla
was just a kid—more than ten years younger
than me. But she wasn't like so many of the
other girls. I guess most of them were a little
overawed by me, by what I'm supposed to
be. Dunno why, because I'm shy myself and
do my best to make other people feel at ease.
But with this chick, it was different. She
didn't give the impression that in any way
she was tongue-tied."

For Priscilla those months they had together in Germany flew by. She saw Elvis

frequently. He was always surrounded by his entourage, always in command, except in his few very private moments with Priscilla. You don't become an idol of millions without a certain charisma, and Priscilla felt its power. She began to regard Elvis as the center of her universe. But she was perhaps too young to see how many of the patterns that would govern their relationship for years to come were being established in those first precious months.

One important element was that they saw each other when Elvis wanted it, not vice versa. The fact that he was in the army and she was just a schoolgirl made this pattern logical. But it was also a reflection of Elvis's views on relationships. His needs came first, and hers were supposed to adjust to that. In *Elvis and Me,* Priscilla revealed that she did find it a little hard to take. Elvis often failed to call when he said he would, and he rarely made plans ahead of time. She would simply wait for the phone to ring, and he would announce that his father would be there to pick her up in an hour or so. Then she rushed to get dressed and ready. It wasn't an ideal arrangement, but she already realized that if she wanted to continue seeing Elvis, she was going to have to learn to accept his way of doing things.

Another element of their relationship that was established right from the beginning was the eternal presence of other people.

Priscilla could be alone with Elvis only when the two of them went into his bedroom, and he never made that move until late in the evening. It gave the time they spent alone in that bedroom, talking and touching, a certain kind of intimacy that might not have developed otherwise. Needless to say, it also gave Priscilla an impatience with the ever-present entourage that she would never lose.

Whatever the drawbacks of her relationship with Elvis, Priscilla was sure of one thing. She wanted to be with Elvis, and she was up against a deadline that she was afraid meant the end of their relationship. Elvis had nearly completed his two-year hitch in the army. He was going to be sent back to the States on March 1, 1960, and then be demobilized at Fort Dix. He would be free to return to the life he had before Uncle Sam called. RCA was planning to release an album as soon as they could get their star in the studio, and they had orders for *a million copies* even before the recording was made. Frank Sinatra had invited Elvis to appear with him on a television special as soon as he returned. And Hal Wallis was anxious to get started with the next Elvis movie, which would be *G.I. Blues.*

Priscilla had every reason to assume that when Elvis went back to Memphis, he would forget all about her. He would once again be worshiped by millions, and Priscilla had already discovered some of the truth about the way Elvis "related" to some of his fans. Red West remembers Elvis in those early days of his fame around 1956: "Elvis then started to relax a lot more when there were gals around. Like everything. When Elvis does something, he goes all the way. Once he discovered how easy he could get girls, we were routing them through his bedroom two and sometimes three a day. That boy sure had a constitution in those early days."

In addition to such dismaying quantity, there were also a few special relationships that Priscilla had found out about. Before he left Memphis to join the army, Elvis had been involved with a local girl, Anita Wood. Priscilla had seen some of her passionate letters to Elvis in his bedroom, and she knew that Anita was just waiting for Elvis to return to pick up their relationship where they had left off.

What Priscilla didn't know was how Elvis felt about leaving *her*. Perhaps Elvis didn't really know, himself. He knew that Priscilla was very special. He had enjoyed the time he'd spent with her, and he wanted her to be there to say good-bye when he left Germany. At the same time he wasn't sure just how serious his feelings about her were. He told a reporter at the time, "She is very mature, very intelligent, and the most beautiful girl I've ever seen. But there's no romance.

It's nothing serious." It seemed that Elvis, too, expected that Priscilla would fade out of his life.

Priscilla still remembers the pain of that parting at the Frankfurt Airport. She rode with Elvis in the car to the airport, and he tried to give her comfort. He urged her to have a good time after he was gone, not to sit around moping. They set up a code so her letters would be sure to make it through the piles of fan mail into Elvis's hands. Just before they reached the airport, he handed her his battle jacket with his newly won sergeant's stripes. "It shows you belong to me," he told her. One last kiss and he was up the steps and into the plane. At the very top he paused and waved to her, and she waved back sadly. Then the doors closed and he was gone.

Priscilla went home, locked herself in her room, and cried for two days.

Chapter 4

A Funny Kind
of Courtship

When Elvis left, Priscilla found herself momentarily in the spotlight. Everyone was curious about "the girl Elvis left behind," and she was interviewed for the first time in her life. She handled the situation well, telling the press, "After all, I'm too young for marriage. But I think Elvis is a wonderful boy—so kind, so considerate and such a gentleman. He gives a girl anything she could possibly wish for." Pictures taken of her with Elvis in the car and at the airport were published in *Life* magazine. The caption read, "Elvis kissed her before he flew to the aid of the girls back home, sorrowful at parting but anxious to get into his bright-colored pants and back to his hip-swinging singing." Years later Elvis's biographer, Albert Goldman, looked at one of those pictures and drew his own conclusions about what it signified. "The picture is of a very young but very pretty girl, one of those young girls who bear already on their faces the unmistakable signs of a woman's beauty. The finely cut lips are parted. The hand is held up in an arrested salute. The feature that rivets the viewer's gaze is the eyes. They are beautiful eyes, nearly innocent of makeup. What is so extraordinary about them is their clouded ecstatic focus, as if they were the eyes of a seer gazing raptly into the future."

The problem, from Priscilla's point of view, was that the future at that moment looked bleak. In her heart she was afraid that she'd never hear from Elvis again. There was his old girlfriend, Anita Wood, waiting for his return. Then she read in the magazines that he was becoming involved with Nancy Sinatra, who appeared with him at a press conference as soon as he returned. Why would he bother with a schoolgirl in Germany? From the very beginning she had asked herself, "Why me, out of all the women he could have had?" Once he left, the question seemed even more unanswerable.

What she couldn't know was how Elvis was feeling at the time. As she had suspected, he was taking full advantage of many of the opportunities that his return to civilian life afforded. But he still remembered Priscilla. According to Red West, he talked about her frequently. "He had another girlfriend at the time, and I won't mention her name because what Elvis said to us all just might embarrass her. But he said, 'It's about time I got a girl who is a bit more sharp.' We didn't know what he meant, but after a while he kept on talking about this girl Priscilla he met in Germany. . . . When he told me she wasn't yet fifteen, I nearly had a heart attack. He assured me that this girl was different, much different from the average Memphis girl, and I was prepared to disbelieve him." All the guys around Elvis noticed how frequently he mentioned Priscilla's name. "Elvis started to talk more and more about this girl as the year wore on. And I believe he even wrote her a letter, which I can tell you is almost unheard of for Elvis."

Red goes on to explain, "A lot of things were happening. We started our movie schedules, kicking off with *G.I. Blues* and . . . we would always bring girls over to him. It's not that we were procuring, but he was still a little shy about making the first approach. That night they would be in bed. That charm, man, it just dripped off him. But he still always got back to talking about Priscilla."

Dee Presley also recognized the seriousness of Elvis's feelings about Priscilla. One day he pulled out a snapshot she had recently sent him from Germany and showed it to Dee. "Check this out, Dee," he said. "You know, I've been to bed with no less than a thousand women in my life. This is the one, right here."

Unfortunately the person who was least aware of Elvis's feelings at this time was Priscilla. All she knew was that she rarely heard from him. He called every few weeks, or every few months, usually at some inconvenient time, such as the small hours of the morning. Although he told her he still cared about her, she didn't know whether to believe him or not. Meanwhile she was sure that he was seeing many other women (and he was). Priscilla told herself that it had just been an interlude... it was silly for a girl her age to expect anything more.

Then, in the spring of 1962, almost exactly two years since she'd last seen Elvis, he called and suggested that she come visit him in Los Angeles. It took weeks to get her parents to agree to the idea. "They were so afraid I'd be hurt," Priscilla recalls. "So was I. I didn't know if the trip was a test, or a trial, or what." But finally it was arranged that she would go for two weeks as soon as school was out in the summer. Her parents insisted that she must be properly chaperoned and that she should write to them every single day, as a sort of check on her whereabouts.

The reunion followed the pattern already established by Elvis for their relationship. Priscilla was met at the airport not by Elvis, himself, but by Joe Esposito. When she finally arrived at Elvis's Bel Air mansion, he was surrounded by a roomful of people who were drinking, playing a jukebox he'd installed, and shooting pool. She recalled the anxiety at that moment. "A maid answered

the door and led me down to the game room.
There was Elvis, with a pool cue in his hand
and a captain's hat on. He rushed over and
hugged me—and I knew everything would
be all right." Elvis gave her an affectionate
kiss but showed no signs of leaving the party
until it broke up long after midnight. He
sent Priscilla up to his bedroom to wait for
him until all the guests had gone. The poor
girl must have felt almost as if she had
crashed the party.

When they were finally alone together, Elvis was all Priscilla had dreamed of: tender,
loving, and obviously glad to be with her
again. Priscilla, who'd had two whole years
to fantasize about this reunion, was ready
for a graceful sexual surrender, but it turned
out that Elvis was not ready to accept it.
"'Not yet, not now,'" she quotes him in her
book as saying in a whisper. "'We have a lot
to look forward to. I'm not going to spoil you.
I just want to keep you the way you are for
now. There'll be a right time and place, and
when the moment comes, I'll know it.'"

Priscilla, then 16, says she was "con-
fused" but didn't argue with him. A more
experienced woman would probably have
understood the warning in that speech
about the future of their relationship—and
put an end to it as quickly as possible. In
Elvis's eyes sexual experience "spoiled a
woman"; the only way Priscilla could have
preserved his romantic feelings was to shut

out the possibility of any sexual connection ever. Moreover, Elvis was also giving her fair warning that he was going to call all the shots in their relationship. Even so intimate a thing as their first sexual experience was going to depend entirely on his decision. It wouldn't be shared. He took it entirely for granted that she would be willing to do whatever he decreed.

Priscilla did her best to regard Elvis's attitude as "romantic," and so it was, if romance can be viewed as just another male-dominated contact sport. She decided that she would enjoy his company for the precious two weeks she could spend with him, and accept his terms. Although she was young, she was not too young to understand that there was something a little strange about his preference. She was also old enough to see that she would have to seem to agree with him if she wanted to stay. So she convinced herself that his insistence on having things his way was a sign of strength. "I like a strong man who will take charge. I couldn't respect a weakling who let a woman boss him around. Elvis is strong and forceful." It's a mistake many women have made at one time or another.

The remaining days of her visit were a whirl of activities. Elvis departed completely from the schedule agreed upon with her parents and took Priscilla off to Las Vegas. (She wrote her daily letters in advance and gave them to someone to post from Los Angeles in the proper sequence.) They stayed up partying and gambling all night and slept all day. Elvis was already using sleeping pills, as well as Dexedrine, to make his abnormal schedule possible. Priscilla was dazzled by the glamour of it all, and excited by the fact that he liked to show her off to his friends. She just continued to be perplexed by the *oddness* of it all.

One of the odd aspects of her visit was that Elvis, although professing his admiration for her natural beauty, began making her over into the kind of artificially attractive woman he seemed to favor. He took her out shopping and bought her absurdly inappropriate dresses, much too sophisticated for her age and much too elaborate for the places she had to wear them. He had the hotel send up someone to fix her hair in an improbable beehive and apply thick black makeup around her beautiful innocent eyes. When Priscilla asked him what had been wrong with the way she looked before, he told her smoothly that it was all right but not the way people looked in Vegas. He seemed delighted by the idea that no one would recognize her as the girl who had arrived just days before. In other words, he wanted her to be *his* creation.

By the end of her two-week visit, Priscilla had almost completely adapted to Elvis's world—even to the point where she had begun to take the same pills he took, so she could stay on that same unnatural schedule. Her hair was teased; her makeup was a thick blanket between her and the world. Despite her occasional uneasy moments with Elvis, she didn't want to leave. He was the one who insisted that she return home on schedule, so her parents wouldn't be angry and refuse to let her go again.

Priscilla's account of her homecoming would wrench any parent's heart. Paul and Ann Beaulieu, who had sent off their lovely 16-year-old daughter for a two-week vacation, were stunned when Priscilla got off the plane. She was wearing one of the dresses Elvis brought her, far too flashy and far too sophisticated to be at all suitable. Her simple teenager's hairdo had been changed into a teased concoction on the top of her head, now collapsed in places from sleeping on the plane. And her young face was covered with heavy makeup, most of which had streaked down her face as she cried her way across the Atlantic. The horrified Beaulieus took Priscilla right home in an angry silence. There was no discussion of the entire episode.

But it wasn't long before the issue came up again. Elvis wanted Priscilla to come to Graceland for Christmas. Once again, her parents were opposed to the idea, and once again, Priscilla's desperate pleading and Elvis's willingness to promise whatever they asked triumphed over parental objections. By mid-December, Priscilla was on her way to her long-awaited Graceland.

Elvis had arranged that Vernon and Dee Presley would meet Priscilla in New York and fly to Memphis with her. He would pick her up at their house and personally drive her through the gates of Graceland for the first time. She *was* impressed, not only by Graceland itself but also by the sight of Elvis on his home turf. Interestingly, the good impression went two ways. While she was marveling over Graceland, the people there were marveling over her. Dee Presley opined, "Everyone was impressed by her. She was a darling girl and quite a young lady. It was obvious to all of Elvis's friends and relatives how well-brought-up she was. She didn't drink or smoke, which Elvis liked, and she had a very easy way about her. She also never made a big fuss about Elvis being a star, which he loved."

Sonny West remembered, "We didn't know what to expect, but we were Southern boys, and a fifteen-year-old girl in Memphis was someone who giggled and talked about a boy's acne. Anyway, that afternoon, just before Christmas, he walked in with her. Man, she was everything he had said she was. She looked much older than fifteen, but not in a cheap way—she was very mature-looking." Sonny was convinced that "she knew nothing about men ... but she seemed

every bit as mature as all of us guys together." (Probably not a difficult feat.) As
Sonny recalls the visit, "It was a very quiet
event. Dinners at home, small parties with
the boys, and I guess we went to the amusement park and the movies, but no wild
times. Priscilla had a very easy way about
her. She had a nice easy laugh. She was
neither overawed with Elvis and the boys,
nor uppity. She was just right. Man, she fit
in perfectly." Sonny concluded enthusiastically, "There was no doubt that Elvis had
got himself a great chick."

Priscilla's warm reception at Graceland
was not lost on Elvis. Even before she went
back home, he began to talk about having
her with him permanently. "The morning I
was supposed to go home, I was sitting with
him in his upstairs office. He told me he
loved me, that he couldn't let me go." The
fact that she was only sixteen he merely re-
garded as a logistical problem. It never occurred to him that it might not be good for
Priscilla. Being with her was what he wanted
and therefore what would be best for everyone.

Shortly after Priscilla returned to Germany, Elvis began his campaign to get her
to come live with him at Graceland.

Chapter 5

☆ ☆ ☆

Priscilla Moves In With Elvis

Back in 1963, it was a very unconventional idea for two unmarried people of any age to live together under the same roof. In the case of Elvis and Priscilla, it was doubly unconventional, because Priscilla was only 16 and still in high school. Whatever possessed everyone to agree to the plan?

Looking back, Priscilla (now the mother of a schoolgirl of about the same age as she was when she moved in with Elvis) says she can understand why her parents finally broke down and said yes. One reason was certainly the enormous pressure from Elvis. She recalls, "Elvis was a strong personality, a man it was very hard to say no to." Red West's brother, Sonny, who also became a member of the Memphis Mafia, explained how Elvis kept trying to get his way. "He spent a lot of time talking to her father on the telephone. Now, Captain Beaulieu was a pretty smart customer. He wasn't suddenly going to let his daughter wander off and take up with a sex symbol, just like that."

According to Sonny, "Elvis really had to pour it on. Elvis told her father that he needed her, loved her and would respect her in every way that her father wanted her respected." (One presumes that this means that he would preserve her technical chastity, a goal he had already espoused for his own reasons.) "He told him that he would marry her one day, and he undertook to put her through school. He would tell us that Priscilla was the one he wanted, because he thought he deserved something better than the girls he was running around with in Hollywood."

The other reason the Beaulieus gave in was the pressure from Priscilla herself. She admits ruefully that her response to the situation was to withdraw from her family entirely. "Elvis and I were both so emotional, and nothing meant anything to me but being with him. I stayed in my room, not caring about my schoolwork, completely unresponsive." The will of a romantic young girl can be incredibly strong, and Priscilla thinks it frightened her parents. "They saw their daughter just breaking apart. They couldn't handle a child who would hate them the rest of their lives. You just can't use logic when you're dealing with an emotion as strong as mine."

So eventually the Beaulieus capitulated. There *were* conditions. Elvis had to send plane tickets for both Priscilla and her father. They would both fly first to Los Angeles, where Elvis was filming *Fun in Acapulco*, and then, after Captain Beaulieu had a man-to-man talk with Elvis, they would go on to Memphis, where Priscilla's father would enroll her in school. She had to promise to finish high school, and Elvis had to promise that she would live with Vernon and Dee Presley, properly chaperoned at every minute.

One can understand why the poor, besieged Beaulieus finally gave in and let their daughter seize what she so firmly believed was her only chance for happiness. But why in the world did the people around Elvis agree to the idea? The potential for damage to his career was enormous. In the several preceding years, two big stars of rock and roll had virtually been ruined by indiscreet dealings with minors. Chuck Berry was arrested, tried, and convicted of transporting a minor, a girl he picked up in Mexico and brought back to St. Louis with him, across state lines for immoral purposes—a violation of what was called the Mann Act. Despite the fact that the girl in question turned out to be a prostitute, Berry was given a five-year sentence and had to serve slightly more than half of it. Shortly thereafter, Jerry Lee Lewis announced his marriage to a 14-year-old girl, and the repercussions were so severe that his career never recovered.

For Elvis to risk public reaction to the fact

that he had imported a high-school girl from
Germany to live with him at Graceland was
extremely foolhardy in the climate of opinion in the early 1960s. Why didn't someone
point this out to him? Where was Colonel
Parker, with his famed concern over Elvis's
image? A few years earlier the Colonel was
in a frenzy about how bad it might look if
Elvis tried to evade being drafted or asked
for special treatment once he was in the
army. Now Colonel Parker apparently registered no protest as Elvis committed an act
that could leave him open to devastatingly
negative publicity at least, and criminal
prosecution at worst.

For publicity purposes the situation was
covered with many coats of whitewash. A
recently published biography conveys the
story the way Elvis wanted it told. "In the
early sixties, Priscilla Beaulieu moved to
Graceland. Her parents were still in Germany, but they wanted her to complete her
education in America. The Presley family
agreed to look after her and arrange school-
ing...and she lived in the east wing of
Graceland, with Elvis's aunt Delta Mae and
his grandmother Minnie Mae. Elvis did not
see her as often as one might imagine...."

Even the whitewash was a rather strange
story to swallow. The truth was much
stranger. As Priscilla explained to an inter-
viewer for TV's *PM Magazine*, she was a
schoolgirl by day and a femme fatale by

night. Her father had enrolled her in the Catholic Immaculate Conception High School, and every morning, she dressed in her schoolgirl clothes, went off to Immaculate Conception (locally referred to as "Virginity Row"), and dutifully followed the nuns' rules of dress and deportment as she struggled to keep her grades up and meet the requirements for graduation. According to Dee Presley, the daytime Priscilla "made friends quickly and easily" and "did the things most normal teenagers do." She was often driven to school in a limo, but after a while, her friends at school apparently forgot the odd context from which she came and accepted her as a friend.

By night, when Elvis was at home, Priscilla's life was quite different. Needless to say, she had moved not just into Graceland but into Elvis's bedroom the minute her father got on the plane to return to Germany. She and Elvis stayed up all night, and whatever they decided to do, they were usually dressed to the teeth. Priscilla's closet was full of elaborate gowns of gold lamé, silk brocade, and black velvet. Each outfit had matching shoes and purse, and some had their own evening coats or capes. Wearing one of these outfits, she might assist Elvis in throwing a party at Graceland for the relatives and the entourage. Or they might all go to the movies—Elvis would rent the entire movie theater for himself and his friends. He did the same thing when they went to the amusement park or the skating rink. Occasionally they would hop on Elvis's private plane and go somewhere for the weekend. Nearly always there was a group— the Guys and their girls—to share in the fun.

This entertainment, although somewhat adolescent, was not completely innocent. Elvis rarely drank, but he was using more and more pills of all sorts to help him sleep when he went to bed as the sun came up, or help him wake up in the middle of the afternoon. And he seemed obsessed with the accessories of violence. He bought a number of guns of all types and even gave a little lady's pistol to Priscilla, which she carried in one of her carefully matched purses. Somehow all that fame and adulation made him feel threatened, insecure. Whenever he went out, his entourage was generally armed and had a backup supply of guns in the car or plane in which they traveled.

It's a wonder that Priscilla managed to cope with the conflicting demands of these two different lives. But she did eventually succeed in graduating (Elvis gave her a little Dexedrine to help her get up for school after the long nights out), and then she was free to spend every day just as Elvis wanted her to. But she began slowly to perceive that it was a life that was going to leave her rather lonely. Dee Presley talked about Priscilla's situation. "She took ballet lessons, but she had to make sure she was right there when Elvis got up or he'd go through the roof. Everything she did was scheduled around him. After a while she hardly went out of Graceland for anything."

But this togetherness rule was abruptly dropped when Elvis wanted to go somewhere without her. He often went away to make a movie or cut an album or make a live appearance, and she was expected to understand that she would rarely be invited to accompany him. According to Elvis's secretary, "Elvis liked Priscilla to stay at the mansion and wouldn't allow her to attend most of his concerts. He would go on the road and she would stay in Memphis." And when Elvis was out on the road, he would continue to entertain himself as he pleased. But, Red West remembers, "He was always careful never to throw up anything in Priscilla's face. Any suggestion that he was playing around was fiercely denied by Elvis. When the gossip columnists started picking up stuff, a lot of which was true, he would deny it outright and call it all publicity and lies." This technique worked amazingly well. "He was very convincing because, by the time the columnists got onto a story about a girl he was seeing, he would be back in Memphis, and he would turn it around that these columnists had him out with a girl while he was at Priscilla's side." Red shrewdly observed that, "When she was younger, I guess she swallowed it, not so much later on. But in those days when he was with her and not running around Hollywood, he was very attentive, very affectionate."

But Elvis's affection never went beyond a certain predetermined point. He stuck to the ground rules he had already established about the sexual side of their relationship. There was plenty of lovemaking but no actual consummation. The two of them shared the same bed every night Elvis was at home, but Priscilla remained a virgin. For some reason that was an enormously important distinction to Elvis, and it almost certainly constituted the basis of his very romantic feelings about her. She was "his," but she was still "unspoiled" and therefore still worthy of his deepest feelings of love.

Meanwhile poor Priscilla was just a young woman in love. When she was snuggled up with Elvis at night, her body was wiser than her brain. It told her that the warmth she felt was good and right and natural and that nothing about it could spoil her. But the decision was not hers to make. Only Elvis could do that.

She also gave in to Elvis on practically everything else. She told reporter Sheila Weller, "If he said, 'That's a terrible color on you,' I'd change my clothes immediately. For years I was self-conscious that my neck was too long because Elvis always told me to wear my shirt collars up. Now I realize...You know all those pictures where *he* had *his* collar up? *He* was the one who was self-conscious about his neck."

Elvis also insisted that Priscilla should always dye her hair the same dark black color he picked for his hair. Sonny West noticed the effect of this hair coloring on Priscilla, and it made him thoughtful. He remembered Elvis's first movie leading lady, Debra Paget, on whom Elvis had developed a serious crush. "If you look at her in those earlier pictures, you will see she had a decided likeness to Priscilla Presley, whom he was soon to meet. She had black hair. When Elvis first met Priscilla, he got her to dye her hair black." Sonny widened his thesis: "I think it's significant that his mother had black hair too. Elvis in real life has very light hair. In that movie you can see he is almost blond. Later on, he dyed his hair black too. Of course, now, when he hasn't had a dye job done on time, his sideburns are almost completely white, like his daddy's."

But it was easier for Priscilla to cope with Elvis's demands—that she wear a certain kind of dress, never eat tuna fish, and be sure to have a regular pedicure—than it was for her to cope with his prolonged absences. Priscilla had so little to do when Elvis was away that it was hard for her to keep her spirits up. Moreover, she worried about what he was doing, and who he was seeing, while he was gone. But she knew Elvis didn't like to hear her complain, so she did her best to keep things bottled inside her.

Dee Presley believes that Elvis was testing Priscilla to see if she was up to the rigors of becoming Mrs. Elvis Presley. "She would wait for his phone calls every day, and Elvis would very often call. But if he didn't, I could tell how let down she was the next day." She was particularly tense when Elvis began filming a movie with Ann-Margret, and the press began to pick up stories of a love affair between them. Said Dee, "I believe she's the only one of Elvis's leading ladies that Priscilla ever worried about. After all, Ann-Margret was a beautiful and very sexy woman, and Priscilla was still in high school at the time." It seems that this was one time that Elvis finally admitted that the rumors were more or less correct. But the affair blew over, and he came back home to Grace-land—and Priscilla—once again.

If Priscilla was something of a caged bird, at least the cage was nicely gilded. She had everything she could possibly want. Elvis gave her cars, clothes, jewelry. When she talked about how she liked to ride, Elvis promptly bought her a beautiful horse. And he didn't stop there. Red recalled how it all snowballed. "It started off with Elvis buying Priscilla a horse. Now she didn't have any-one to ride with, so Elvis bought his cousin Patsy Presley a horse so she could ride with her. Then he bought himself one. And when he saw us looking on forlornly at them riding horses, he decided we all should have horses. He bought every one of us a horse." Next came the cowboy outfits for everyone, with genuine Stetson hats and fancy leather boots. Within a few months Elvis had bought a ranch to go with all the horses, and then he started buying four-wheeled jeeps and trucks for everyone, and trailers for them to live in on the ranch. In the end, Priscilla's horse had set off a million-dollar spending spree.

But for Priscilla it was somewhat off-target. It wasn't so much the things she wanted as it was the intimacy with the man who gave them. And he was often completely preoccupied with other things. Sonny West explained, "It was like everything he does. He got what he wanted, put it away in storage, and went on to something else. Priscilla could have had anything she wanted. But the thing she wanted most was Elvis."

Chapter 6

☆ ☆ ☆

Elvis and Priscilla
Get Married

Years later Dee Presley told a reporter her thoughts about Priscilla and Elvis in those years they lived together. "It was wild for those days, but Priscilla kept in the background, and no one knew about her. I just remember thinking, 'When's the wedding? When are they getting married?'"

If Priscilla was thinking the same thing, she never told anyone. But maybe she did tell Elvis ... or at least find a way to let him know what she wanted. Sonny West recalls that Elvis and Priscilla had their battles, many of them about other women. "They had fights, like any normal couple, but she had a mind of her own. She had suspicions that he was running around with other women, but she never really caught him in the act. She was not going to be made a fool of, I can tell you."

Elvis and Priscilla argued about his other women, about the time he did or didn't spend with her, and possibly about his commitment to the relationship. Says Sonny, "I always got the feeling that in the early days, Priscilla didn't like us hanging around as much as we did. She never said anything, but I guess she had arguments along the line that he spent more time with the boys than with her." Sonny remembers one fight in particular. "This argument was really a beauty. He was ranting and she was really screaming. We were about three bedrooms away, but you could hear furniture and things falling all over. Elvis comes out, and he is extremely calm for someone who has been ranting and raving. He said quietly, 'I just told her to pack all her stuff and get out.' At this time he is helping her pack, throwing her clothes out of the closet onto the floor. Well, she is all packed and he walks in and says to her, 'Now unpack, goddamn it, you are not going anywhere.'" It was an impressive demonstration of his power over her. Sonny understood the nature of the message Elvis was delivering. "He could make a person feel very insecure with that sort of stuff; he did it with us all the time, making you think that you were not in as tight as you might have thought you were...."

It was not surprising that Elvis didn't want to change their relationship (except to make sure that Priscilla remained docile). He, after all, was having his cake and eating it too. He could leave anytime he wanted to, for as long as he liked. And if he exercised only a reasonable amount of discretion, he could see anyone else he wanted to. He had Priscilla confined in Graceland, simply waiting for him to decide that he would return to her. When he did, she was prepared to drop everything and devote her entire time to making him happy. She saw that the house was run the way he wanted it, that his food was cooked (or overcooked—Elvis liked things half burned) just right. She stayed up with him all night, and when he got up the next afternoon, she was gamely ready to do whatever he wanted. She would ride motorcycles, scoot around in golf carts, let him dress her like a doll for every appearance outside their bedroom. Best of all, he was able to have sexual affairs with other women and still keep Priscilla on a pedestal as the unspoiled girl he loved best.

There was no doubt about the love he felt for her, and that, of course, was what Priscilla responded to, what made her willing to put up with everything else. The fact that his love imposed some odd conditions didn't really make it any less romantic to her. Perhaps, instead, it emphasized the fairy-tale quality of their relationship. After all, fairy-tale princesses are always being faced with strange demands: They must stay shut up in a tower all their lives or take a frog to bed or marry the first man who can make his way up the glass hill to snatch the apples from their laps. Priscilla, who has referred to her life with Elvis as a "pure fantasy," was willing to view Elvis's demands as one more inexplicable element of her fairy-tale existence.

Priscilla almost surely wanted to marry Elvis, but she just as surely didn't have the power to force his decision. Another woman in her position might have tried emotional blackmail, such as threatening to leave if he didn't propose, but Priscilla was not the kind of person to play that game. She suffered from a strong streak of honesty, and besides, she was simply too much in love with Elvis at that time to consider leaving him.

More important to the outcome of the situation was the question, "How did Elvis Presley feel about marriage to Priscilla?" Elvis had a very romantic outlook on life. To him marriage was the ultimate commitment, true love forever, the kind of feeling his daddy had had for his mother. He wouldn't enter into it lightly, because he expected it to endure for the rest of his life.

There was also a question about whether marriage was the right step for Elvis professionally. He was the fantasy boyfriend of millions of women of all ages who might become discouraged if he turned into just another married man. On the other hand, he was no longer a kid but a man pushing into his thirties.

It seems, from all reports, that Colonel Parker came down firmly on the side of marriage. From the time Elvis got out of the army, the Colonel had been trying to push his career in the direction of the cultural mainstream. It's all very well to be a teenage idol, but teenagers are notoriously fickle. One day they love you and the next they have embraced your replacement, and suddenly you're yesterday's news. Not only that, teenagers constitute a minor segment of the population, and they don't have the buying power of their elders. And then, of course, there was the fact that Elvis was getting on, even getting gray. How much longer could he expect to hold his position as the King of rock and roll? The Colonel was thinking about all these issues and pushing Elvis in the direction of attracting a larger and older audience. Doing his army hitch helped, as did some of his appearances on his return, such as the TV special with Frank Sinatra. Even the material he was recording was moving into the cultural mainstream, with more slow ballads turning up amid the rock. The Colonel thought it was time that Elvis became a solid citizen. And what could symbolize that step better than taking a bride?

There are those who claim that the Colonel masterminded the marriage and railroaded Elvis into it. But the available evidence suggests that all Elvis needed was a gentle push...just the reminder that it was the right time and Priscilla was the right woman. Elvis *did* love her, and his romantic vision of their marriage was always somewhere in the back of his mind. The fact that it coexisted with other visions of his freewheeling life-style didn't trouble him.

Elvis proposed to Priscilla just before Christmas, in 1966. He did it quite formally and, as you might guess, very romantically. So sure was he of her answer to the question that he had the ring in his pocket, ready to put on her finger. It was a beautiful creation, with a three-carat diamond in the center, surrounded by a detachable border of twenty smaller diamonds. For Priscilla the whole thing seemed like a dream come true. In fact, everyone at Graceland basked in the couple's happy glow. Dee Presley shared her memories of the event. "They called me upstairs, and I had no idea of what was going on. They were sitting side by side on the couch and Elvis was holding her hand. She was wearing the ring. I was so happy I kept saying, 'Oh, my goodness! Is this what I think it is?' And they were laughing."

Once that romantic personal moment was over, the Colonel took charge of the situation. He was concerned that the wedding plans had to remain a deep dark secret until minutes before the ceremony, because he feared the whole thing would be overrun by the press and fans and get totally out of control. Moreover, he obviously wanted to make sure that the wedding was conducted in a way that middle America would approve of, producing pictures that would generate more and better publicity for Elvis. He so strongly impressed Elvis with the need for secrecy that Elvis agreed to turn all the arrangements over to him. It's understandable that Priscilla felt somewhat regretful over that delegation of what is usually the bride's role.

The Colonel wouldn't tell Elvis and Priscilla when and where the ceremony would take place, but he did instruct Priscilla to go ahead and pick out her dress and have everything in readiness. By Elvis's standards the dress she finally chose, in a store in Los Angeles, was alarmingly simple. Floor-length organza, it was altered to add a six-foot train. The dress was made in the Empire style with a high waist; the bodice and long lace sleeves were trimmed with seed pearls and bugle beads. It was a pretty wedding gown rather than a striking one, and quite becoming to the petite bride. With her dress in readiness all Priscilla had to do was wait until the Colonel told her when the wedding would be.

The plans were finally made by the middle of April. The foxy Colonel wanted Elvis and Priscilla to go to his house in Palm Springs at the end of the month. Family and some friends would gather there, to throw the reporters off the scent. The night of April 30,

Elvis and Priscilla would hop in a plane, fly to Las Vegas, apply for a marriage license in the wee hours of the morning, and get married in Vegas a few hours later. Speed was of the essence, for once the news of the marriage license got out, the press would begin to descend on Las Vegas.

Everything went smoothly, according to the Colonel's plan. The couple signed the marriage license application in the office of the County Clerk at 3:30 A.M. on the morning of May 1. The cost of the license was fifteen dollars. Elvis gave his age as 32, Priscilla as 21; they both said they were legal residents of Memphis. The Colonel then arranged for them to be driven to the Aladdin Hotel, whose owner, Milton Prell, was a long-time friend of his. After a brief rest it was time to change for the wedding. With her gown Priscilla wore a fluffy three-quarter-length tulle veil that was held in place by a double-tiered rhinestone crown. Her hair was teased into an enormous bubble, augmented with a few hairpieces for good measure. What with the hair, the crown, and the veil, she looked nearly as tall as the groom in the wedding pictures—despite the fact that she is slightly under 5′4″ tall. She carried pink rosebuds on a white leather Bible, and she was attended only by her sister Michelle. According to one published report, when Elvis saw her at the altar, he whispered, "You look like a fairy queen."

Elvis was wearing a black brocade coat and vest with plain black pants. His dress shirt was completed by a black bow tie, and he wore a white carnation in his lapel. He had not one but two best men: Joe Esposito, who acted as his road manager; and Marty Lacker, his accountant. According to Dee Presley, he was decidedly fidgety when the moment of marriage came.

The ceremony was performed by a Justice of the Nevada Supreme Court, and it was over in just eight minutes. Elvis gave Priscilla a diamond band that fit into her engagement ring, and she gave him a plain gold band in return. (It was later lost somewhere on the grounds of Graceland and never recovered.) At her request the traditional vows had been slightly altered. "Love, honor, and obey" were changed to "love, honor, and *comfort.*"

Colonel Parker had arranged for the actual ceremony to take place in Milton Prell's personal suite on the second floor of the hotel. Then, at the last minute, he informed Elvis that the suite was so small, it would not be possible to have more than fourteen people present at the ceremony. That meant that there was room for family only. Vernon and Dee Presley were there, and Dee commented that "Priscilla was just radiant in her white organdy dress. Nobody could take their eyes off her."

Priscilla's family was also there. Her father, by this time a major in the Air Force, was stationed at Fort Ord, in northern California, and Elvis sent tickets for her parents and Michelle and her oldest brother, Don, to come to the wedding. Priscilla later told Elvis's secretary, Becky Yancey, "I think Mother was happy to get out of the house for a few days. One of my brothers had just gotten out of the hospital, the washing machine went out, and the plumbing wasn't working right when they left home. Of course, they were happy for me. They were starting to wonder, because Elvis and I had been dating for years." That was certainly a tactful way of putting it. No doubt her parents had been wondering what would happen next, but it's by no means certain that what they hoped for most was a wedding. By this time they had probably seen and heard enough to realize that marriage to Elvis Presley wasn't necessarily a guarantee of a lifetime of unalloyed happiness for their daughter.

What concerned Elvis at that particular moment was the number of people who *weren't* there. Most of his entourage—the Guys, who had spent most of their time for years in his company—were conspicuously absent. The Colonel said smoothly that it was unavoidable because the room was so small, but, of course, Elvis realized that that only begged the question about why the ceremony was held in such a small room to

begin with. Colonel Parker assured Elvis that
everyone else would be at the reception immediately following the wedding, but in fact,
some of the uninvited had already taken of-
fense and left.

According to some accounts, Red West was
so angry that he was on the verge of thrash-
ing Colonel Parker with his own cane. Red
later spoke plainly about his feelings about
the situation. Before the event he had been
told to go to Vegas, check into the Aladdin
Hotel, and wait for further instructions
about the wedding itself. He, his wife, Lamar Fike, Charlie Hodge, and a few other of
the Memphis Mafia were gathered in eager
anticipation of this big event in their bud-
dy's life. "I'm sitting in my room and there
is nothing happening. No telephone calls,
nothing. So I go down to Joe Esposito's
room, knock on the door, and he is all
dressed up in his tux. I ask Joe what's going
on. How come nobody has told me what time
we're going to the wedding? Now Joe looks
like he has swallowed a frog, and he tells
me, 'You all aren't going to the wedding...'"
The news really staggered Red. "The man
brings us all the way to Las Vegas, and then
we are told that we're not invited to the wedding. I suspected Joe and the Colonel had
fixed this up. And Elvis wasn't being
thoughtful enough to make sure what is
going on. Boy, was I mad!" Red heard the
news of the wedding on television and

promptly packed his bags to go back home.

According to Priscilla's own account of her wedding day, Elvis was himself extremely upset when he realized how few of the people closest to him would be present at the ceremony. The responsibility for the unpopular decision seems to rest squarely on the shoulders of the Colonel, and it's not immediately clear why he deliberately excluded many of the people who had been part of Elvis's entourage for years. Perhaps he hoped Elvis's marriage would be a time for his protégé to break away from the group life-style he had forged with all the good old boys. Or perhaps he was afraid that the Guys would disrupt the solemnity of the occasion with practical jokes and horseplay. Or maybe he just enjoyed the opportunity to emphasize the fact that he was the one who had the power to call the shots in any situation. Whatever his motives, the result of his plans was a great deal of tension for everyone attending both the wedding and the reception. The strain was undoubtedly greatest for Elvis, who, of course, realized how angry his friends were going to be about the whole situation. It wasn't a particularly auspicious start to Priscilla's married life.

Things did loosen up a bit at the reception after the ceremony. The reception consisted of a breakfast for one hundred people that reportedly cost ten thousand dollars. Elvis never ate anything for breakfast but bacon and eggs, and you can certainly buy a lot of bacon and eggs for that amount of money! In actual fact, there was free-flowing champagne, roast suckling pig, oysters Rockefeller, and good old Southern fried chicken. Colonel Parker was the official host of this event, which was perhaps suitable, given his standing as spiritual father to the groom. Some members of the press were invited to the reception, although they were asked to leave their cameras outside until after the meal. Official photographs of the entire event were later released to the media. The highlight of the reception was the cutting of the wedding cake, a five-foot creation decorated with pink rosebuds to match the ones Priscilla carried and inscribed with the names of Elvis and Priscilla. A string ensemble strolled around the room and serenaded the guests, frequently playing some of Elvis's most famous ballads. At one point they surrounded the bride and saluted her with "Love Me Tender," which seemed an appropriate gesture.

At the end of the event the Colonel had arranged a press conference. It is not recorded that Priscilla said anything... but then, even on her wedding day, she was not the true focus of interest. Dee Presley summed it up tartly. "Priscilla knew what she was stepping into. Elvis's career came first. Elvis's fans came first. Then came

Priscilla. She was told to stay in the background. She understood that."

Elvis confided in reporters that being a groom made him feel more uncomfortable than anytime since he first appeared on *The Ed Sullivan Show.* To questions about where he met Priscilla, which indicated how well her existence had been hidden for four years, he answered that he'd known her in Germany. He explained that they would continue to live in Memphis and added that they hoped to "spend a lot of time on my new horse farm in Mississippi."

One reporter asked the question that everyone wanted to know—perhaps even the bride. *Why Priscilla?* Elvis gave an interesting answer. "Priscilla was one of the few girls who was interested in me, for me alone. We never discussed marriage in Germany. We just met at her father's house, went to the movies, and did a lot of driving—that's all. I waited for her to grow up." Aside from the fact that he has taken the liberty of moving their meetings from his house to hers and rather naturally omitted any mention of all those hours they spent privately in his bedroom, he probably gave as truthful an answer as he knew how to give. He did believe that Priscilla was interested in *him* rather than in his fame or his fortune. And he was quite right. She would have been quite happy—maybe even happier—if he gave up his career and stopped showering her with cars and jewels but instead settled down with her at Graceland. It wasn't exactly a vine-covered cottage, but it would do for a substitute.

There was one more ritual moment to come for the new Mr. and Mrs. Presley. That was the wedding night. For years Elvis had been jealously guarding Priscilla's virginity, thus keeping her "unspoiled." Now that he had finally chosen to marry her, that game had to come to an end; even Elvis could see that. The pressure surrounding the final consummation of their years of sexual excitement must have been immense. Priscilla had been looking forward to this moment for almost as long as she could remember, a fact of which Elvis was naturally aware. The length of time she'd waited, plus the way Elvis talked about the importance of putting it off until it could be right and perfect, must have generated very high expectations. Any man would be somewhat apprehensive about his ability to live up to those expectations. Priscilla thought she detected real signs of nervousness as the moment approached.

The couple flew back to Palm Springs in a Learjet that belonged to Frank Sinatra, and Elvis carried Priscilla over the threshold of his house there. (According to Priscilla, he was singing "The Hawaiian Wedding

Song" at the time.) Before the sun went down, they were alone in Elvis's bedroom, which was dominated by a king-size bed.

It is greatly to Elvis's credit that Priscilla had indeed decided that it had all been worth waiting for. It was a very special event, one whose intensity lingered in her memory even fifteen years later, when she sat down to write her book about her relationship with Elvis. She says emphatically, "As I went from child to woman, the long, romantic yet frustrating adventure that Elvis and I had shared all seemed worthwhile. As old-fashioned as it might sound, we were now one. It was special. *He* made it special, like he did with anything he took pride in."

Chapter 7

Being "Mrs. Elvis"

Priscilla Presley was probably one of the most envied women in the world in 1967, rather like Lady Di was to be more than a decade later. She had snapped up one of *the* most eligible bachelors, and press reports seemed to highlight his devotion to his new bride. Her youth and beauty made her a generally sympathetic figure to many fans, and most of her mail at that time was favorable. There were a few angry letters to Elvis, as well as occasional threats of suicide now that he was married, but most of his mail, too, was favorable. His secretary recalls, "Some people around Elvis were worried that the marriage would damage his swinging image. There was no need to worry. Many of Elvis's female fans are married and have children or grandchildren. They were thrilled when Elvis married. And most of his teenaged followers were understanding. Priscilla was barely out of her teens herself, and as Elvis's young wife she was someone with whom many of the young girls could identify. We received letters from many of the girls pledging their continued loyalty to Elvis and condemning any fans who deserted him now that he was a married man."

Would those millions of women still have envied Priscilla if they knew what it was really like to be Mrs. Elvis Presley?

At first married life must have seemed wonderful to Priscilla. She was no doubt disappointed to discover that their honeymoon, which Elvis had boasted to reporters would last a whole month, ended in just four days because Elvis began to get fidgety in Palm Springs and to think about all the other things he could be doing. In just a few weeks they returned triumphantly to Graceland where they hosted a big reception for all the people who hadn't been able to attend the wedding. Priscilla and Elvis donned the same clothes they were married in, there was a new and equally elaborate cake to cut, champagne flowed freely, and Graceland itself was lit up and decorated to the hilt. There was a huge buffet and an even huger gathering of congratulatory guests. Once again Priscilla seemed radiant, and Elvis seemed uncomfortable. This sort of large ceremonial occasion always made Elvis nervous; he didn't have the social background to take it in his stride.

After all the festivities were over, Priscilla settled into her new role of lady of the manor.

Redecorating was the order of the day. She turned first to Graceland, which had evolved over the years into a cluttered mess of mementos from friends, relatives, and fans. For example, nearly every tabletop was covered with crocheted doilies sent to Elvis by loving fans. Priscilla wisely got rid of the doilies, as well as many lamps, ashtrays, and knick-knacks. She ordered new curtains and carpeting to make the rooms look better coordinated, and she installed china cabinets to display the silver pieces she and Elvis had received as wedding presents. She redid her own dressing room and bathroom in shades of pink but was careful not to turn their bedroom into a room that reflected only her tastes. She told secretary Becky Yancey, "The bedroom for a husband and wife should never be too feminine. It's better for it to be more masculine. It's important to please the man. Elvis would never be happy with anything pink and lacy. And I couldn't be happy living with him if he's not happy." According to Becky, Priscilla didn't enlist the services of a decorator but bought moderately priced furnishings at local Memphis stores, including Sears.

It seems that Priscilla initially threw herself into the role of homemaker. When she and Elvis went to the Mississippi ranch he had bought at the height of his horse fever, she enjoyed doing all the housework personally. She washed Elvis's clothes, ironed his shirts, and cooked his favorite breakfast of bacon (at least a pound) and eggs every morning. At Graceland she planned the menus and supervised the staff. Then, shortly after her marriage, she had a new house to think about. Elvis sold the Los Angeles house where Priscilla had first visited him and bought a bigger one, in fashionable Holmby Hills. He paid $400,000 for the house itself, and then invested at least half that much in redecoration. This project gave Priscilla a chance to exercise more of her own taste, with attractive and comfortable results.

For a while Priscilla's dreams appeared to be coming true. She and Elvis were spending time together, and the Memphis Mafia was less in evidence than it used to be. The ranch was a good getaway place, and Elvis seemed to enjoy its simple pleasures.

But then things slowly began to fall back into their old patterns. The Guys began to reappear, and Priscilla was unhappy about their continual presence. "Somebody's always there, everywhere we go. A bunch of guys and their wives are always around. We never have any privacy." A long-awaited trip to Hawaii with Elvis turned into just another excursion with the Guys. In their book, Red and Sonny West showed their understanding of the strain this put on Priscilla. "The boys never really got close to Priscilla. Not that she was standoffish; she wasn't.

She was extremely pleasant. But they respected her position, and also they didn't want to exaggerate their already noticeable presence to a woman who perhaps couldn't be blamed if she wanted more of Presley to herself." But the fact that they understood the problem didn't solve it.

At the same time that Priscilla felt Elvis didn't spend enough time at home alone with her, he also began to go away more often. Most of his absences were connected with the problems of his career. For, in the late 1960s, although Elvis was still the King of rock and roll, there were getting to be an awful lot of princes. First there was the so-called British invasion, led, of course, by the Beatles and the Rolling Stones. Then came a new resurgence of American pop music with the Beach Boys, Jefferson Airplane, the Doors, the Byrds, Janis Joplin, and the Grateful Dead. Elvis's albums still sold but not in the numbers they used to. Even his movies weren't drawing big crowds anymore. Elvis Presley was beginning to look perilously like a thing of the past.

The Colonel's antidote was to arrange for NBC, the network affiliated with Elvis's record label, to give Elvis a Christmas special on television. At first Colonel Parker insisted that it should be like every other Christmas special ever made, with Elvis singing all the old favorite holiday songs while standing in a fake blizzard. But the producer, Steve Binder, saw a possibility of something much more exciting. Binder's principal credit was a 1965 production, *The T.A.M.I. Show,* which featured everyone from Chuck Berry and James Brown to Mick Jagger and Jan and Dean. Binder believed he could do a whole show about Elvis himself, dissecting his roots, displaying his casual charm, letting his real musicianship come through. He and his camera crew spent hours shooting film with Elvis just talking, and eventually the star got over his natural stage fright and began to act like himself—the funny, attractive personality his close friends knew and loved. Binder also managed to create a sort of jam session between Elvis and a group of talented musicians with the same roots in gospel and rhythm and blues. To nearly everyone's surprise it showed Elvis at his musical best and brought back the sense of urgency that had been such a part of his early success. And Binder finally won over the Colonel on a key point; instead of closing the show with a hoary Christmas favorite, they used a new song Binder had commissioned just for the special. It was "If I Can Dream," which turned into one of Elvis's greatest hits.

That special was a turning point in Elvis's career, which slowly began not so much to revive as to expand. The TV show was eventually followed by Elvis's first live appearance in Las Vegas, and that introduced Elvis to a whole new venue of performing, put him squarely in the cultural middle ground where the Colonel wanted him. In a way it almost seems that Elvis was born to star in Vegas. He had the right combination of real talent and tacky spectacle. He began to appear in those outrageous costumes made of leather and studded with silver or rhinestones. There was usually an exaggerated collar that came up to the middle of his ears and enough chains all over to suggest a love of bondage. Priscilla was the one who thought of adding to this costume a cape, with its connotations of Superman and Dracula. Elvis just loved to walk out on the stage with that cape flowing behind him. It made him feel larger than life.

These live appearances took Elvis away more and more frequently. Priscilla tried to be a good sport. "Sure, I wanted to go with Elvis when he would leave for location to work on a new movie or go on the road for a series of performances," she told Becky Yancey. "But I understood that I had to make adjustments. Elvis had to learn to live with his work, and so did I." And, in fact, when she did go with him, she found life on the road to be mostly a boring wait for Elvis to wake up and decide to do something. He had always preferred to sleep in the day and live at night, and working in Vegas kept him more or less permanently on that schedule. Priscilla, spending most of her time as a homemaker, was on the opposite schedule, and it was increasingly difficult for her to stay up all night with her husband. A few scary experiences with the pills Elvis gave her for that purpose convinced her to stop taking them.

But even when they were together, Priscilla felt a growing emotional distance between herself and her husband. A lot of it had to do with Elvis's worries about his career. He felt increasingly threatened and vulnerable. He feared both losing his fame and running out of his fortune—in short, losing his throne. But he couldn't share that sense of vulnerability with anyone. Priscilla commented sadly, "Most of the time he held all that tremendous vulnerability in... And he insulated himself from his own feelings too. Whenever he was scared, or doubtful, or guilty he'd say, 'I can't feel that way.'"

Elvis couldn't express that sort of feeling to the Guys, because he thought they expected him always to be a strong leader, the King. He couldn't express it to the Colonel, because the Colonel might have taken advantage of Elvis's weakness to exert even more control over his life and career. He couldn't express it to his father, because he felt Vernon looked to him for reassurance. The West brothers give an example. "His old man, Vernon, would just gasp when he got those bills [for Elvis's purchases]. Elvis would laugh and say, 'Hell, man, there is plenty more money where that came from.'" That was the persona he had established with all the people around him; he could scarcely reveal that he, too, worried about whether he could really continue to earn the large amounts he had in the past.

Above all, Elvis couldn't express any of these vulnerable feelings to his wife. The pattern of their relationship had been set when she was a 14-year-old girl and he was a world-famous idol. He was the all-powerful figure who had arranged her life, made her decisions, taught her how to dress and behave, offered her a fantasy life that only a star of his magnitude could create. She was expected to heed his commands, accept his decisions, give him first place in everything. How could he then turn to her in the middle of the night and admit that he was frightened?

Many years later Priscilla discussed the fact that Elvis had in many ways been a father figure to her, and a rather suffocating one at that. "Eighty percent of my life with Elvis was good, but I'd begun to realize there was a world out there, outside of his protection. He'd dominated everything I did. He was not only a lover but a father to me, and as long as I stayed with him I could never be anything but his little girl." The sad part of it all is that Priscilla would have *liked* to see the relationship change. She wanted to grow up, and she wanted to be a real partner to her husband. She was quite willing to share his worries and anxieties, and the fact that he had them would not have diminished him in her eyes. But Elvis was trapped in his own very old-fashioned definition of the roles of husbands and wives. He was ready to provide for Priscilla and protect her, but not to turn to her for help.

Billy Stanley was an astute observer of Elvis as a husband. "Elvis was always very protective of the women in his life. That's how he loved and took care of them. Vernon and Elvis were both like that—really strong Southern gentlemen—no swearing in front of their women and everybody around them treated them with respect . . . They had to do everything in the world for their women; the women never had to ask for anything because it was given to them before they could even ask for it. The main thing was that the women never did a lot of striving for themselves—there was always somebody there. That's the way Elvis treated Cilla. . . ."

When the role of protector and provider seemed too demanding, Elvis did sometimes escape by taking refuge in the role of a child. He didn't know how to be an equal partner in a relationship, but when the problems of being the father figure were too much for him, he would sometimes turn into the baby. Pat Perry, who was one of the few women allowed in Elvis's entourage back in the 1960s, accepted as something like a kid sister, told a reporter about that side of Elvis's personality. "Elvis wasn't really a man's man, even though he was around these Southern macho guys. He was a woman's man. Besides this incredible person onstage, there was also the little-boy Elvis who used to talk baby talk and the Elvis who needed somebody to pat him when he was hurt. He needed babying after his mom died."

So sometimes, with Priscilla, he recreated the magical world of childhood he had enjoyed as his mother's treasured son. He called his wife "Sattnin," which had also been his pet name for his mother. He used baby talk with her that he had used with his mother: "sooties" for feet, "itty-bitty" for anything that could be remotely considered small, and so on. During these periods of psychic collapse Priscilla found herself mothering Elvis. This abrupt shift in roles must have been a bit bewildering. Yet it was apparently part of Elvis's appeal for women, a theory that Albert Goldman expertly advanced: "Once Elvis was past his first romantic infatuation with a woman, the character of his relationship with the woman began to change radically. The erotically charged emotion of the initial phase would vanish, and in its place would arise a totally different kind of connection. Instead of passion, the theme would now become play. Instead of heavy macho wooing, the roles would reverse and the woman would be expected to take the initiative."

Apparently this pattern was established in many of Elvis's early romances, and according to Linda Thompson, the girlfriend who eventually succeeded Priscilla, Elvis behaved much the same way at the end of his life. Goldman writes, "Soon...Elvis would slip into his basic role, which was that of a child being babied by his adoring mother. It used to astonish the Guys how swiftly this transformation could occur: how a girl whom Elvis had dated just a few times would suddenly start mothering him and speaking to him in baby talk. He struck a chord in women, all right: the umbilical cord."

It was probably a sign of the respect Elvis felt for Priscilla that he was less likely to revert to this childish behavior with her than he was with the other women in his life. Still, it was one more sign of his reluctance to grow up.

That reluctance, and his own insecurities, kept Elvis, and Priscilla with him, isolated in a fantasy existence. Priscilla often speaks today of the dangers of being "in a bubble," and her awareness of those dangers obviously sprang from her life as Mrs. Elvis Presley. As she explained after Elvis's death: "There was no newness, no outside world at all." Nothing impinged on Elvis's private world. Some of Elvis's critics believe that isolation is what killed him. An article in the *Village Voice* put that thesis very forcefully. "An exile from the real world, Elvis Presley built his own world, and within it—where the promise was that every fear, every pain, every doubt and every wish could be washed away with money, sex, drugs and the bought approval of yes-men—Elvis Presley rotted. It was a fantasy of freedom with the reality of slavery...."

As Mrs. Elvis Presley, Priscilla had to share much of that isolation. But already she had an instinct to try to make contact with the real world. It's remarkable, really, since she had been living with Elvis from the time she was only 16. He had conditioned her to accept his view of the world, molded her to be a full partner in his fantasy life. Yet somewhere deep inside she knew that fantasy could be dangerous and self-destructive. In the time she had to herself, she began to make an effort to escape the confines of her fairy-tale existence.

One of her first efforts came through her study of ballet. It started simply as a way to kill time, something to while away those long periods when Elvis was gone and she had little to do. She enrolled in dance classes in Memphis, and she found that she enjoyed it. In addition to the actual dancing itself, there was the freedom of entering another world, and a very disciplined one at that. Becky Yancey recalls how Priscilla felt. "We were in the office one day answering fan mail when the door flew open and Priscilla bounded inside, leaping and pirouetting gracefully around the desks. . . . Finally she shifted one leg, swept one arm behind her and ended the impromptu performance with a bow. 'Ballet!' she explained. 'These are some of the steps I've been learning.'"

She kept on with her dancing lessons, and she even danced in several recitals. She used an assumed name, so people wouldn't come to see Elvis Presley's wife; that wasn't the kind of recognition she wanted. She would rather be just another obscure aspiring dancer than the wife of a famous man.

According to Becky, Priscilla also managed to model at fashion shows in Memphis, again using an assumed name. "She attended the Patricia Stevens Finishing School and modeled for a while at the Picadilly Restaurant not far from the mansion, and at a local store. All most diners were aware of when she glided out to show an outfit was that she was a lovely dark-haired model."

Friendship was another way that Priscilla could try to fight against her Elvis-imposed isolation. Circumstances prevented her from making friends outside the tight circle of Elvis's entourage, but she did manage to get to know some of the women in the circle and counted them her friends. Becky Yancey was one of them. Becky was only five years older than Priscilla, and they often had lunch together. Elvis's cousin Patsy was another friend. Patsy was in fact a double first cousin: Elvis's father's brother Vester had married Elvis's mother's sister Clettes—a not uncommon occurrence in the rural society where they lived. Elvis and Patsy had grown up together, playing together and even having asthma attacks together. At the time Priscilla came to Graceland, Patsy had recently married Marvin "Gee Gee" Gambill, Jr., who was Elvis's chauffeur and wardrobe master. Patsy, like Priscilla, had time on her hands at Graceland, and the two women often did things together. Joe Esposito's wife, Joan, was another friend of Priscilla's, and she sometimes shopped with her and advised her about housekeeping matters.

It was necessary for Priscilla's mental health to have a few friends around her that she could talk things over with, to relieve both the isolation and the boredom. In many ways she was even more isolated than Elvis, because he was necessarily out in the world because of his career, but he believed that women should be at home, waiting for their menfolk. According to Elvis's stepbrother, Billy Stanley, "That's what Elvis liked about the whole arrangement. He always loved the idea of having a woman back home waiting for him." Priscilla did her best to share that point of view. Billy's brother Rick recalls, "When Elvis and Priscilla were first married, she used to love to call him 'my husband.' She really enjoyed being Mrs. Elvis Presley, and Elvis loved her in that role. They both felt very privileged to have each other."

For Priscilla it was a privilege that came at a high emotional cost. Looking back, she says, "It was a lifestyle so outrageous that I'm just thankful I've come out sane."

Chapter 8

Becoming Parents

When Priscilla and Elvis were married, she had expected it to be the start of a truly shared life and looked forward to all the things they were going to do together. "I had so many dreams with Elvis," she confessed years later. "We were going to travel everywhere together, things we couldn't do before because we weren't married." And at first they did in fact manage to go a few places together. According to the West brothers, Elvis and Priscilla traveled to the Bahamas soon after the wedding. "He thought it would be another Las Vegas, but when he got there, he didn't like it. He was particularly disturbed at what he believed was the tense racial situation. So he went on to Hawaii with Priscilla and Joe Esposito and Jerry Schilling. Presley had wanted to go to Europe, but the Colonel dissuaded him, because he did not want to take the luster off Presley should he ever do a tour of Europe."

Priscilla was no doubt disappointed that

these early trips didn't turn out to be more successful, but she was willing to bide her time and try again. As she told Andy Warhol, "With my father being in the Air Force, I traveled around all my life. I think that's why it's hard for me to confine myself to one place. I love to travel."

But travel with Elvis, as it turned out, was a pleasure she would rarely be able to experience. Several months after the wedding, Priscilla discovered that she was pregnant. "When I found out I was pregnant so quickly after the marriage, I had mixed emotions." That must have been an understatement.

Physically Priscilla's pregnancy was quite normal. Emotionally it was anything but. Priscilla rather naturally had hoped for some time alone with Elvis, time for them to get adjusted to marriage and time to change the patterns of their previous existence. And it had seemed as if they were off to a promising start. They went to the ranch to be alone together, and the Guys had either left the entourage or kept their distance from the newlyweds. But Priscilla was afraid that motherhood would change everything once again.

She had, in fact, discussed birth control with Elvis as soon as they were married. She wanted to take the pill, but he was opposed to the idea—on the grounds, he said, that it might be risky for her. Presumably he was opposed to other methods as well. At any rate, it was only several months after their first real lovemaking that Priscilla began to suspect what had happened. She talked to Patsy, already a mother, who confirmed that Priscilla's symptoms were probably those of pregnancy. Then she went to a doctor, who made the diagnosis definite. A baby was on the way.

Priscilla must have been very anxious about telling Elvis. He had never expressed any particular desire for children; moreover, a child would represent another emotional demand laid on him before he had even grown used to the new demands of marriage. Would he feel, as she did, that it was really too soon to start a family?

Of course, Priscilla had one other reason to worry about the effect of her pregnancy on Elvis. She must surely have been aware of his feelings that motherhood was a sexual turnoff. He had mentioned it on numerous occasions; and no doubt she'd already been shrewd enough to guess that there was some connection between his desire to keep her "unspoiled" for all those years and his lack of desire for women, however beautiful, who were mothers.

Priscilla must have dreaded telling her husband the news. Yet he actually took it very well. In fact, he soon began acting like the normal expectant father: helping to choose names and daydreaming about the future when the family had expanded to three. He was making a movie that summer, *Speedway,* and his co-star, Bill Bixby, told journalist Jerry Hopkins how Elvis appeared to him at that time. "Bill Bixby recalls that after he found out Priscilla was pregnant, he was ecstatic. Bill says Elvis always wore his wedding ring, right up to a take, then put it into his pocket, replacing it afterward. 'He seemed totally content. I remember him whistling and humming. He was thinner, and everything seemed to be falling in place.'"

One reason that Elvis took the news of Priscilla's pregnancy so well was her effort to suppress all the outward signs of it. She dieted rigorously so her pregnancy wouldn't show. Becky Yancey recalls, "Only two or three months before Lisa's birth, her mother looked almost as slim, petite and stylish as if she were not pregnant. Priscilla never wore maternity clothes. She didn't have to." She lathered herself with cocoa butter in the hope of avoiding stretch marks, and she never, *never* complained about any of the unattractive problems of being pregnant, such as swollen feet or backache or morning sickness. Whatever it cost her, she kept silent. That was the price she had to pay if she wanted an attentive and happy father-to-be. Elvis could accept the situation only as long as he didn't have to deal with the physical reality of it.

While she waited for the baby, Priscilla gave serious thought to the way it ought to be raised. Talking to Becky Yancey, she said, "I don't care if it's a boy or a girl. But I'm not going to have my baby spoiled by being given everything it wants. If you want to build character, you have to teach children that it takes effort to earn the good things." She was aware that the baby would have a special problem because of the fame of its father. "I know that people are going to love it because it's Elvis's baby. But I want the baby to have a normal childhood, and it's not going to be that way if presents and everything it wants are just heaped on it. I don't want him or her just settling for living off Elvis's name."

Obviously a big part of her worry was what kind of a father Elvis would be. She knew how he liked to lavish presents on everyone around him and how he could be at once doting and demanding. She hoped Elvis could just be an "ordinary" father to his child. She talked to him about it, and he understood her point. But she was asking him to be something he wasn't. Nothing about Elvis was ordinary, and fatherhood wasn't going to be any exception.

Elvis laid detailed plans for getting Priscilla to the hospital with all due speed at the same time that they avoided alerting the press or the fans. Elvis always enjoyed these exercises in secrecy and seemed downright disappointed whenever someone made him aware that they weren't strictly necessary. Elvis and Priscilla were to be driven to Memphis's Baptist Memorial Hospital in one car, while a big black limo, driven by some of the Guys, was supposed to draw off any attempted pursuit. A backup car was held in readiness, in case either of the new Cadillacs broke down. The hospital had been alerted to provide a private room for the waiting entourage, and some off-duty policemen had been engaged to guard the mother and her baby.

The big event began early on the morning of February 1, 1968—nine months to the day after Priscilla and Elvis were married. Everyone got to the hospital quickly, although something went wrong with the elaborate plans for deceiving the fans, who chased Elvis and Priscilla the entire way. Once they all arrived, there was nothing for anyone to do... except Priscilla. In those days it was customary for laboring mothers to be sequestered somewhere in the depths of the hospital while fathers simply waited nearby, passing the time as best they could. Even with the entourage to distract him Elvis was nervous and anxious as he waited for news. In the middle of the afternoon he went home to change his clothes so he would be ready to meet the press afterward.

The baby finally arrived at 5:01 P.M. She was a girl, named Lisa Marie Presley, and she weighed six pounds, fifteen ounces. Elvis, Vernon, and Dee immediately went to the maternity ward to see her. According to Dee, "She just picked up her head a little and looked at us with those blue eyes, and Elvis's face lit up like a beacon. I've never seen him look like that in all the time I've known him." Shortly afterward the trio went to visit Priscilla. "Cilla was still groggy from the anesthetic," says Dee. "She couldn't believe she really had a baby girl—it wasn't sinking in. Once she began to grasp it, she just sighed and looked so peaceful."

Elvis retired to the waiting room to smoke a cigar with the Guys. He was too keyed-up to deal with the public. He asked his father to go cope with the waiting press. "Tell them I'm a happy but shaky man," he instructed. Vernon gave the waiting newspeople the essential details, including her name: "No special reason for it. They picked it out of a baby book." A few days later, when Elvis took his wife and new daughter home, he faced the press himself, "Oh, man, she's just great," he said enthusiastically. "I'm still a little shaky. She's a doll, she's great. I felt all along that she'd be a girl."

Shortly after the little family returned to Graceland, Elvis was off again, back in Hollywood making another forgettable movie. Priscilla found herself once more on her own. But now she had a baby to look after. Everyone at Graceland agreed that Lisa Marie was a very special baby and that Priscilla was a wonderful mother. Dee Presley recalls: "Lisa Marie was a frisky baby. She was just like her mother in many ways. Her mother really knew how to take care of her and not spoil her, like Elvis did." For the moment Priscilla was content to devote herself to her child and her domestic responsibilities. She later reflected, "I was totally devoted to my life-style at that time, to being a wife and mother. I had no ambitions then. It was a totally other life." Dee Presley's views reinforced this point. "She was having to stay in so very much. Her life was like mine—very sheltered—just getting up, going to the dance studio, and coming home. Elvis slept during the day when he was home, so they never got to go out."

After the birth of Lisa Marie, Priscilla was even less likely to accompany Elvis on his trips than before. The hours he kept, the life he led in hotel suites, the drugs, the entourage, the groupies—it was a life-style ludicrously unsuitable for a small child. And Priscilla didn't like to be separated from her daughter while she was still so young, so she didn't want to travel without her. The situation made it easier and easier for Elvis to lead his own life and be on his own whenever he chose. Linda Thompson, who insisted on going on the road with Elvis when she became his girlfriend in the early 1970s, saw the difference in the way Elvis treated his wife. "Priscilla was the role of wife-mother, tucked away in a corner somewhere. She never went on the road with him. She came to Vegas at first on the weekends and after a while that stopped. Elvis told Priscilla, 'You don't take your wife to work with you.'"

Priscilla had constructed her own emotional defenses about the situation. A former member of the entourage explained, "When I was talking with her in Vegas, she told me, 'I just come up two or three times while he's working here. I don't stay here and bug him. I just know he has to do his thing and be alone at certain times.'" He went on to comment, "It's a mature attitude to take. It's the only way she could have a successful marriage with him."

Meanwhile she did have the pleasure of Lisa Marie's company. And when Elvis came home, he threw himself into the role of doting daddy. He loved to wax sentimental about his daughter. In an interview with May Mann he said, "Lisa means more to me than my life. She is my life. I'll do everything to make her happy and to protect her." He described his daughter as being "petite, like her mama ... but oh, so smart!" In Elvis's mind, making people happy was synonymous with giving them presents. He lavished gifts on his daughter: clothes, toys, a pony cart. It taxed his imagination to think of what to get a small child—his customary gifts were cars and jewelry—but he did his best.

Unquestionably he loved his daughter dearly. In the book Dee Presley wrote with her sons they said, "She brought out a side of Elvis unlike any other, and the very wonder of her existence could make him meek as a lamb. You could see his passion for her rise up in his expression when she was an infant and he would return from Hollywood or Las Vegas and dawdle lovingly over her bed to recite prayers, or when he would sing her lullabies and envelop her with the love of his voice. Sometimes the mere sight of her could make him cry." But the role he preferred was the giver of gifts, the provider of treats. When it came time for real discipline, he left that to Priscilla. Dee speculates, "He just didn't get to take her to the zoo and to the park and do the things that normal daddies do. So Elvis had a tendency to let Lisa have her way much more than Cilla did." Day in and day out, it was Priscilla who worried about the child's schedule, her health, her psychological well-being.

Understandably Priscilla worried about bringing up her daughter. Children of famous people are unfortunately likely to be emotionally handicapped by growing up in the shadow of a famous parent. Some people they meet try to exploit the famous connection; others put down the child for

lacking the parent's gifts. When you add to
that problem the fact that Elvis tended to
spoil his daughter by giving her everything
she wanted before she could even realize that
she wanted it herself, you can understand
Priscilla's concern. She said firmly, "I want
Lisa to have as normal a childhood as possible, but she won't if everything is just
heaped on her without her having to exert
any effort. She is Elvis Presley's daughter—
nothing can change that—but neither Elvis
nor I want her to take advantage of anyone
or anything because of her name." She went
on to reflect, "All fathers tend to spoil their
daughters, and Elvis is no exception. By
comparison, I'm the disciplinarian—but I
don't mind. We both want Lisa to have the
best, but there is a limit. There's got to be."

In the same interview Priscilla also revealed a glimpse of the way young Lisa felt
about her father. "Lisa adores her daddy and
has a great respect for him. When she sees
him on TV, she is so proud. I try to take her
to Las Vegas whenever Elvis performs there."
Everyone agreed that father and daughter
had a very special bond. Many people
thought they even looked alike. Priscilla
comments, "The press always says that she's
an Elvis look-alike. But unless you know her
name, I don't think you see that resem-
blance." In the most recently published picture of Lisa, she looks more like her mother
than her father—except for the eyes, which

Priscilla Beaulieu Presley kisses her new husband at the conclusion of their wedding ceremony in Las Vegas on May 1, 1967.
AP/WIDE WORLD PHOTOS

Priscilla seems to be examining her three-carat diamond ring, while Elvis looks suitably impressed by the seriousness of the occasion.
AP/WIDE WORLD PHOTOS

Nine months to the day after their wedding, Elvis and Priscilla become parents. This was the first official photo of the Presley family after baby Lisa Marie made it a threesome. AP/WIDE WORLD PHOTOS

Elvis and Priscilla leaving the California court → *where their divorce became final. Only days later, Elvis would enter the hospital for detoxification.*

AP/WIDE WORLD PHOTOS

In 1971, the Jaycees honored Elvis as one of the ten Outstanding Young Men of the Year. Although the marriage was already in trouble, Priscilla dutifully accompanied Elvis to the Jaycee's Prayer Breakfast. AP/WIDE WORLD PHOTOS

Priscilla is wrapped up in a South American boa constrictor in this 1980 publicity photo for "Those Amazing Animals," the ABC-TV show she co-hosted with Burgess Meredith and Jim Stafford.
AP/WIDE WORLD PHOTOS

Wella corporation announces that Priscilla is to be the spokeswoman for their hair-care products.
AP/WIDE WORLD PHOTOS

Priscilla stayed close to Elvis's dad, Vernon Presley, and she and Lisa visited him in the hospital when he was treated for heart problems. AP/WIDE WORLD PHOTOS

Priscilla is snapped by a photographer at an airport as she embarks on one of the long trips she loves to take. AP/WIDE WORLD PHOTOS

*Priscilla strongly identifies with her Dallas charac-
ter Jenna Wade; this publicity photo was taken
after Jenna went to prison, where she was given a
functional haircut.* AP/WIDE WORLD PHOTOS

Priscilla and Mike Edwards return from a short trip to South Africa. AP/WIDE WORLD PHOTOS

←*Priscilla gets all dressed up to attend a banquet honoring Dallas producer Leonard Katzman. Next to her is Audrey Landers, who played Afton.*

AP/WIDE WORLD PHOTOS

Priscilla Presley today: poised, confidant, and her own woman at last. AP/WIDE WORLD PHOTOS

do resemble her father's in that downward slant that always made Elvis's expression look so sultry.

There are in fact very few pictures of Lisa that have been published. One point on which her parents were always in complete agreement was the need to protect Lisa's privacy. Elvis was continually—almost obsessively—concerned about the threat of kidnapping. He feared that the daughter of one of the most famous men in the world was a natural target for ransom demands, and he made sure that Lisa was always well protected. At Graceland she was well guarded and protected by the elaborate security system there. When she traveled, some of the Guys were usually along, and they were customarily armed. With his exaggerated fear of kidnapping Elvis certainly was not going to put ideas in anyone's head by publishing pictures that would help malefactors recognize his daughter.

Priscilla's concern was a little different. She wanted to make sure that her daughter had a sense of privacy that would allow her to live her own life freely. Priscilla herself had been dismayed by the fact that photographers were frequently hovering about, just waiting to snap a candid shot of Mrs. Elvis Presley, whatever she was doing. She didn't want her daughter to suffer from the same invasion of privacy, and one way to insure that was to keep Lisa as unrecognizable as possible. Most of the pictures that have been released show Lisa at a younger age than at the time of publication, so they won't reveal her current appearance. Priscilla's care on that point continues to the present day. In her own book she included many photos of Lisa as a child, but the only one that shows her as a teenager is taken from so far away (and Lisa is also wearing a concealing hat) that it is impossible to tell what she really looks like. Her caution seems to be necessary. Tabloid photographers regularly try to track Lisa down and photograph intimate moments with friends and boyfriends. And occasionally there are scary incidents when someone follows Lisa for days or makes threats on the telephone.

Despite all the problems of Lisa's father's fame, most of her childhood days were secure and happy. She played all over the thirteen acres surrounding Graceland. She had a pony and three cats. Best of all, she had her constant companion, Snoopy. Snoopy was a Great Dane, one of a pair that Elvis had bought for Priscilla. Priscilla loved animals and was extremely fond of her dogs, but once Lisa came along, it was obvious that she and Snoopy were soulmates, and he became her dog rather than Priscilla's. Priscilla said in an interview, "They understand each other completely. Some adults have trouble with Snoopy, but Lisa just gives a command and Snoopy heels in a hurry."

Christmas was always a very special occasion in this little girl's life, thanks in large part to her father's enthusiasm for holiday gift-giving. Every year he saw to it that Graceland was decorated like fairyland, gladly paying huge bills to light up the whole outdoors in his excessive holiday spirit. He loved to receive presents himself and always opened everything under the tree for him, even when the packages numbered in the hundreds, thanks to the devotion of his fans as well as family and friends. David Stanley, another one of Elvis's stepbrothers, talks about some of the happy memories that Lisa must retain of her Christmases at Graceland. "Elvis really felt good around Christmas, because he would get off on doing the whole number for Lisa. He'd wait up all night long on Christmas Eve so he could be waiting downstairs first thing in the morning when she got up, and he'd play Santa Claus for her. Those were some of the closest moments between him and his daughter."

Those efforts Elvis made to please his daughter inevitably touched Priscilla's heart. Elvis might have been a poor disciplinarian, but in some ways he was a wonderful father—loving and generous and always admiring, an important boost to a young girl's developing self-image. Priscilla never ceased to give Elvis full credit for his virtues as a father. Even after they were divorced and she had gone on to another life, she made a touching confession in an interview. She remarked that she didn't think she'd ever have another child, whatever the future might hold for her. The reason? "I don't think it would be fair to the other children if Elvis wasn't their father too."

Chapter 9

A Marriage in Trouble

Unquestionably Priscilla and Elvis were happy parents. They both loved their daughter Lisa Marie very much, and they shared the pleasure of watching her grow and change. Although Priscilla tried hard to keep Elvis from spoiling their daughter, she gave in on holidays and let Elvis do as he pleased. And Elvis, in his turn, usually recognized that Priscilla's rules really were in Lisa Marie's best interests. He was sometimes disappointed when Priscilla told him not to give his daughter so many valuable gifts and not to let her do absolutely everything she wanted to. But in his heart he understood that his wife was probably right, and he never undermined her maternal authority.

But if Elvis and Priscilla were in agreement as parents, it was the only area of their relationship that was going well by the late 1960s. As husband and wife they were having serious problems. Elvis was preoccupied first with a Christmas television special in late 1968, and then with his dramatically successful return to live performing at the International Hotel in Las Vegas.

By the early 1970s he was touring again, almost as much as a decade earlier. Once again, he was away most of the time. Priscilla was left at home with the baby, dutifully awaiting his occasional visits. Elvis wanted her there when he came back home . . . but he wanted to be the one to choose when he would come and how long he would stay. Sonny West said, "In the last couple of years she was with him, he was away from her eighty-five percent of the time. She wouldn't see him for several weeks at a time. Then they would spend the weekend together, and then he was out again. She could buy all the clothes and jewels she wanted and Elvis would not have said a word, but she didn't want that. She was not a heavy spender when you think of other girls who have been around him. She just wanted a normal life."

The slip backward into that old familiar pattern must have been very disillusioning to Priscilla. She'd had the romantic hope, common to many women, that marriage would somehow change things between her and her husband. In fact, the only thing that had changed was the painful deterioration of their relationship.

One of their chief problems at this point was sexual. Elvis had never made any secret of the fact that he didn't like to make love

to women who had borne children. Most Elvis observers agreed that this revulsion was
somehow tied to his deep feelings about his
own mother; psychologists recognize this as
the "Madonna or whore" complex. Whatever
the cause of this attitude in Elvis, it was too
strongly rooted to change when he got married and became a father. Priscilla was now
the mother of his child, and apparently that
permanently removed her from the category
of sexually attractive women.

In an interview with a British journalist
in 1984, Priscilla Presley revealed that Elvis
had made love to her no more than fifty times
in the course of their marriage. In her book
she says that they continued to make love
passionately until the last six weeks of her
pregnancy, so simple arithmetic tells us that
the number of times they made love *after*
the birth of Lisa Marie must have been very
small indeed. Priscilla was in the unhappy
position of being envied by women the world
over because she was the wife of an international sex symbol... with whom she had
almost no sexual relationship.

Priscilla wrote frankly of the hurt she felt
over this situation in her book, *Elvis and
Me*. She admits that as months passed after
she became a mother, she felt more and more
anxious about the missing sexual element
in their marriage. She even did her best to
seduce him, using the classic ploy of the
black negligee and some open advances (ap-

parently unusual in their relationship). Elvis's response was to fall asleep.

Elvis understood that Priscilla was upset,
but apparently he was unable to alter his
deep-seated aversion to mothers as sexual
partners. Perhaps he lacked a real incentive
to change because there were always other
women available to him; they virtually threw
themselves at him. Meanwhile he tried to
appease Priscilla by telling her that being a
mother of his child was a very special position. Priscilla did her best to accept that
point of view with its implicit corollary: "So
don't expect anything else." But she was an
attractive young woman, not yet 25, and her
relationship with Elvis had always had a
strong physical component. Suddenly she
found herself shut out from physical intimacy and even sexually rejected by her husband. In her book she gladly quotes a diary
entry she made during this time that gives
some indication of the effect Elvis's behavior
had on her: "I am beginning to doubt my
own sexuality as a woman. My physical and
emotional needs were unfulfilled."

Years later she explained another aspect
of the problem of her marriage. "With Elvis
my life was his life. He had to be happy. We
never disturbed him. My problems were sec-
ondary." It's possible to live that way for short
periods, but Priscilla began to understand
that that was to be the script for her entire
life.

Sonny West noticed that "Priscilla was gradually getting more and more annoyed. He kept her in a doll's house, an ivory tower. He didn't want her hanging around the movie locations because he heard that Hal Wallis, the man who produced most of his movies, had said he would offer her a movie contract anytime she wanted it." But Elvis didn't want his wife to have a career. "A woman's place was in the home, looking after her man—when he was home." Elvis rarely was.

Left on her own for long stretches of time with little in the way of intimacy to look forward to when she *was* with her husband, Priscilla needed to find ways to keep herself busy . . . and to keep herself from being psychologically devastated. Although she could have become a "Hollywood wife," filling up her time with endless rounds of shopping, beauty treatments, and lunches with friends, it is to her credit that she aspired to something more challenging. She took dancing lessons, learning both jazz and ballet. Later she began taking private art lessons. Both helped to give her the sense that she had abilities of her own, could accomplish something in her own right, wasn't completely swallowed up in the role of "Mrs. Elvis Presley."

But she still had time on her hands. It was Elvis who suggested that perhaps she could fill that time by taking karate lessons.

He had been interested in karate for years and had even used some karate moves in his Vegas show. Priscilla thought that perhaps if she took it up, it would be something they could share.

Following her husband's suggestion, Priscilla enrolled in a karate school owned by Chuck Norris and Ed Parker. In addition to karate she also studied Tae Kwan Do, a ritualized, almost balletic version of the sport, which she found both demanding and satisfying.

Sometime late in 1971, Priscilla began to take lessons with one of Chuck's associates, karate expert Mike Stone.

Mike Stone was a native Hawaiian. Like Elvis, he became acquainted with karate while in the army. When his military hitch was over, he competed professionally; in 1966, he was an international grand champion. Although he had married and retired from active competition by the time Priscilla met him, he was still in great shape, a natural athlete who took good care of himself. Priscilla thought he was an attractive man, and a nice one—a view shared by many other people.

Dee Presley recently told a reporter, "I can't really blame Priscilla for a lot of things. . . . She thought she was something special being Mrs. Elvis Presley but it wasn't exactly the best thing in the world to just sit in the house while Elvis was the center of attention all the time. She gave it her best. She tried. Then she openly rebelled...." Her "rebellion" was to become emotionally involved with Mike Stone.

Priscilla's growing involvement with Mike Stone was paralleled by the continued deterioration of her marriage to Elvis. He was touring most of the time, and he made it clear that he didn't want his wife to accompany him. He was less and less careful about covering up his frequent involvements with other women.

When they were first married, according to Memphis Mafia member Sonny West, "He would give the girls the cold shoulder whenever Priscilla was around. He gave Priscilla a lot of respect, but there is no doubt that Elvis wanted to have his cake and eat it too." As time went by, the truth of that remark became more obvious. Rick Stanley explained that Elvis frequently managed to cover up the situation by attributing the presence of other women to the members of his entourage. "He had nine other guys covering for him. It was up to us to go down with the ship and accept the fact that we were caught, but save the Boss! Don't let it get to where Cilla gets on him. Sometimes he would be completely lost for words and he would look at us with an expression on his face that said, 'Come on, man, say something! Help me out!'"

Sonny especially remembered one particular episode when Priscilla and a few of her girlfriends went to spend a few days of rest and relaxation on their own at Elvis's house in Palm Springs. There they found a number of letters in the mailbox addressed to Elvis and his entourage. The contents of the letters unfortunately made it clear that Elvis and his companions had been entertaining female companions in this weekend hideaway. An especially revealing message to Elvis that said, "Let's do it again," was signed "Lizard Tongue." Priscilla was understandably upset about Lizard Tongue. According to Sonny, "Priscilla got on the telephone and crawled all over Elvis, and she wanted to know who Lizard Tongue was. There were so many girls around then, I'm damned if I remember who it was who was supposed to be Lizard Tongue. Elvis was laughing his head off, but when Priscilla started to crawl over him, he got right back at her and turned it around where she was almost apologizing for calling him. He told her that she should be more intelligent than to take anything like that seriously with all the crazy fan mail he gets. I don't really know whether she believed it."

Elvis's stepbrother Rick Stanley had his own opinion. "I'll tell you something: nobody ever pulled the wool over Cilla's eyes. She *knew;* she knew the man better than anybody and was aware of the situation. She knew Elvis had other chicks and that he was an entertainer and that was part of it, but I could see that she couldn't accept the fact."

Priscilla's own book makes it abundantly clear that she wasn't fooled; moreover, that she realized exactly how Elvis manipulated the situation to try to make her feel in the wrong for asking the question. She felt tired of living that way.

Accounts of Christmas at Graceland in 1971 make it evident that Priscilla was already beginning to cut her emotional ties to Elvis and his life-style. The holiday celebration went on just as usual. The house and the long driveway were sparkling with thousands of tiny lights. Presents were piled under the tree in the living room. On many evenings Elvis rented the local movie theater to watch films of his own choosing, including such un-Christmassy titles as *Diamonds are Forever, Straw Dogs,* and *Dirty Harry.* Whatever happened to peace on earth, goodwill to men?

Priscilla did her best to keep up the facade. She went to some of the movies and she spent a lot of time with Lisa Marie. But Elvis's secretary, Becky Yancey, remembers that Priscilla once came into her office and asked her to mail a couple of gaily wrapped packages addressed to "Mike Young," and she also remembers a conversation they had in Becky's office. Riffling through some mail, Priscilla remarked sadly, "Marriage seems to change everything. People seem to forget about the other person's needs after they've been married for a while. They don't do things because they want to anymore, or because it's fun, but because they have to or they're expected to. Elvis and I were so happy together before we got married. It's more fun being a girlfriend than a wife."

Elvis went ahead with his usual lavish gift-giving. He wanted to give Priscilla a car, but she pointed out that he'd given her a beautiful chocolate-brown Mercedes just the previous year (he bought five others for friends at the same time). He settled for giving her ten one-thousand-dollar bills. Journalist May Mann says that Priscilla told her, "Elvis was more than generous. I could have all the money to spend I wanted, have any and everything I wanted. But what can you do with closets full of clothes and no place to go to wear them? Elvis gave me beautiful jewelry—but you don't wear jewelry around the house. . . . Elvis was gone much of the time on tour. When he came home, he was enveloped with his recording and business people." Priscilla concluded, "I wasn't happy with his life, although I loved Elvis."

According to a report by rock journalist Jerry Hopkins, it was at a party that Christmas that the strains of the marriage became evident to the people around them. Priscilla was beautifully dressed in a black-and-white ankle-length gown with a long slit skirt that revealed expensive tall white leather boots.

When Elvis walked over to her to see if she needed anything, she answered with a curt negative and then turned her back on him. Elvis became silent and morose. Hopkins says, "It was as if Priscilla virtually ignored Elvis as she chatted amiably and somewhat smugly with some of the wives present, hinting at an affair that Elvis still didn't suspect. 'This,' Priscilla told the girls, 'was the year I came out.'"

If anyone there was puzzled by the remark, all they had to do was wait. Only a few weeks later Priscilla made herself unmistakably clear.

Chapter 10

☆ ☆ ☆

Breaking Up

In show business, marriages like the Presleys' in 1971 are not at all uncommon. The star, concentrating on a career at its zenith, travels a lot, drops out of ordinary family life, has affairs with co-stars and one-night stands with fans. The consort appears on state occasions, such as an opening in Vegas or the night of the Oscars, and spends the rest of the time out of the limelight, decorating and redecorating the houses and taking care of the children. These consorts take their diversions where they find them, and everyone understands. Meanwhile the marriage goes on, because it brings benefits to both sides. The image of a stable home life is good for the star and acts as a protection against paramours who want too much too soon. The consort gets the money and the life-style that many people dream of. Both accept the emotional emptiness as part of the compromise.

That's what many people expected Priscilla Presley to do. If she had discovered that she was in love with Mike Stone, all well and good, but it's no reason to break up a marriage. Especially one in which the two parties saw each other infrequently. Sonny West comments, "She could have screwed around on him. I remember one night I came back from Las Vegas unexpectedly and was at the house. She came in and was shocked to see me. I looked outside and Mike Stone was driving her Mercedes. Priscilla was a bit embarrassed and said, 'You remember Mike, don't you?' We shook hands. She knew that I knew she was going with Mike, and she knew I hadn't informed on her, so she was secure. If she had wanted, she could have kept up that double life as long as she liked."

But Priscilla Beaulieu Presley was not like other show-business consorts. Rather than continuing to lead a double life, she put an end to it as soon as possible. She decided that she would leave Elvis to live with Mike Stone. Rick Stanley explained, "That's just the way she was. Cilla never cared about what other people might think when she did things as long as she truly believed in what she was doing." Sonny West put it more succinctly: "She didn't want to make a fool of Elvis. I liked her for that."

Priscilla left because she was an honest person, uncomfortable with the necessity for long-term deceit. She also left because she

craved emotional and physical intimacy...
intimacy that she had lost with Elvis and
hoped to regain with Mike Stone. She told
secretary Becky Yancey, "When we're together, it's just the two of us. We don't have
a gang of other people around all the time."
After all the years of literally living with the
Memphis Mafia, Priscilla especially appreciated the privacy she found with Mike. She
confided in Becky, "Mike's very masculine.
He treats me like a woman, and he never
lets me forget that he is a man." That, too,
must have been a welcome change for Priscilla. Elvis's stepmother, Dee Presley, also
spoke right to the point when she said, "Mike
was an extremely beautiful person... it's as
simple as that. I could understand how she
could be in love with him. He was self-
assured, quiet, friendly, and very hand-
some; most important, I think, was that he
really made her feel like a woman. She felt
a real commitment from him which she felt
lacking with Elvis, and the chance to lead
a more down-to-earth normal life."

Biographer Albert Goldman makes the interesting point that Mike Stone was the reality of which Elvis was the facade. Elvis was
appearing in Vegas wearing a costume pat-
terned after a karate master's, incorporat-
ing karate kicks and hand moves as part of
his choreography. He liked to present himself as a man's man, tough and virile. But

in reality he was by this time living on drugs and dependent on the cocoon provided by a twenty-four-hour-a-day entourage. And although he seemed to want to take a woman to bed every night, he generally used her as a teddy bear rather than a sex object; by the time he was willing to leave the warmth of his entourage's care and devotion and be alone with his choice of the evening, he was usually so tired and so drugged that he fell asleep before anything passed between them but a few words of endearment. And, of course, in Priscilla's case, after she became the mother of his child, things usually didn't even go that far.

In Mike Stone, Priscilla found a man who was genuinely tough and virile, and sure enough of it that he was able to open himself up to tenderness and intimacy. At one point, when Priscilla was still just a teenage kid and Elvis a famous star, she had hoped that she'd found those qualities in him. Later, around the time of their marriage, she hoped that he would develop them. But by the early 1970s she had apparently accepted the fact that she would have to find them in another man. She later explained to Rick Stanley, "Ricky, I'm a woman. I need somebody there." Mike Stone said much the same thing to Albert Goldman. "We made love very often. It wasn't just a desire for sex—it was love. Priscilla was starved for affection. She was warm and loose and funny. She was born again."

Matters came to a head in February of 1972, when Priscilla went to Las Vegas to see Elvis's show at the Hilton Hotel. According to some accounts of the incident, Priscilla went there with her mind made up, just looking for the opportunity to tell her husband she was leaving. Priscilla herself describes it as a decision made on the spot, after Elvis asked her to come up to his suite and grabbed her and made love to her forcefully and crudely, utterly unlike his usual gentle approach (and, of course, also unlike his recent policy of no approach at all). Whether or not she was already thinking about making her announcement, that brief encounter seems to have been a deciding factor.

There is no doubt that Elvis took the news hard. In the past he had used threats of sending Priscilla away as a method of keeping control over the relationship, and she had never once retaliated. Now he could scarcely believe that she was really serious about breaking up the marriage. According to Priscilla, Elvis said, in shock, "I don't believe what I'm hearing. You mean I've been so blind that I didn't know what's going on? I've been so wrapped up, I didn't see this coming."

Ed Parker said Elvis came to him to talk about the split and started crying. "She has everything money can buy, Ed—cars, homes, an expense account. And she knows that all she has to do is ask and I'll get her whatever she wants. I can't understand, Ed. I love that woman." To Red West he said, "I tried to give her all the freedom I could. Sometimes a man and a woman have to have their own lives." But what Priscilla wanted was something that money couldn't buy, and it had nothing to do with her freedom. She wanted a real partnership with the man she loved.

On February 23, 1972, Priscilla moved into an apartment of her own, a modest two-bedroom near the ocean for which Elvis gladly paid $50,000 in decorating bills. "I remember standing in the living room of the apartment . . . watching the movers set down the cartons, thinking, 'My God, can I *do* this alone?'" But she wasn't entirely alone. A month later Mike Stone's wife sued him for divorce. Within months she was awarded their house and custody of their two children, along with a reasonable monthly sum for alimony and child support. Mike Stone was free to move in with Priscilla.

It seems that Priscilla did not initially tell Elvis that she was involved with Mike Stone. Although Mike was surely the catalyst for her departure, he was just as surely not the cause. That lay deep in the Presleys' failed marriage. Red West claims he was the one to tell Elvis about Mike Stone's affair with

Priscilla; other accounts have Elvis learning the truth from the maid. Interestingly, Elvis seemed not to hold this relationship against Priscilla, but he was immediately wild with anger against Mike Stone. In Elvis's world-view men were the competitors and women were the trophies. He didn't see any reason to blame Priscilla for being stolen by another man.

The West brothers say that Elvis was so worked up about the situation that he wanted Mike Stone dead. According to them, he tried to hypnotize Sonny into doing this task for him. Telling Sonny to look into his eyes, he repeated over and over in a monotone, "The man has to die. You know the man has to die, the son of a bitch must go. You know it, Sonny, you know it. There is too much pain in me and he did it. Do you hear me? I am right. You know I'm right. Mike Stone has to die. You will do it for me— kill the son of a bitch, Sonny. I can count on you. I know I can." The Wests say this sort of behavior went on for days. Once Elvis went to his closet and came out with an M16 rifle and pressed it in Sonny's hand; later he suggested that Red should get in touch with someone in organized crime and arrange for a hit. Red West says that he did eventually make the call. "Now, what I did, I'm not going to make a whole lot of excuses, apart from the fact that I loved the guy and just couldn't stand seeing him hurt so bad.

And let me tell you, he was hurting." But eventually Red was able at last to impress on Elvis the reality of what he was talking about, and Elvis finally let the matter drop.

Rick Stanley doubts that Elvis was ever really serious about the matter. "That was all talk," he says. "Elvis was just blowing off steam. Elvis Presley was *human*. To a certain extent he did feel that his wife was stolen from him, but he also knew that he'd messed up and accepted the consequences. Sure, sometimes he'd get angry as hell, as much at himself as at Mike Stone, and he'd say things like, 'Man, I'd like to blow that guy away....' The proof that it was all talk is that Mike Stone is alive and well today."

Albert Goldman interviewed Mike Stone, who said he thought at the time that the death threats were ridiculous. Perhaps it was Priscilla who was meant to be the real target of Elvis's remarks. Goldman recounts a phone call from her estranged husband that made Priscilla nearly hysterical. She hung up and told Mike that Elvis had said that "he's flying down here from Las Vegas with the Guys, and he's going to make me watch while he makes you get down and crawl."

Dave Hebler, a black-belt karate champion who was soon to be on Elvis's payroll, thought that part of the problem was the blow to Elvis's pride. He remembers seeing Priscilla, in a pair of jeans, at a tournament with Mike. "So this is Priscilla Presley and here she is, stamping hands at her boyfriend's tournament. She was just helping out her struggling karate instructor boyfriend, who I guess in those days in a good week would have been making $250. Maybe that was what bugged Elvis so much. If she had run off with someone like Frank Sinatra, maybe, somehow, that would have eased the hurt ego. I don't know. But a 250-buck-a-week karate instructor, that must have hurt."

Elvis himself downplayed the extent of his reaction. He later told journalist May Mann: "I wanted to get my hands on Mike Stone and kill him—that was my first reaction. That's rational indignation. My anger cooled, and I forgave them. Priscilla is the mother of our child and I will always be her friend."

Oddly enough, while all this drama was going on over Mike Stone, Elvis and Priscilla seemed to be working out the details of their separation in a generally amicable fashion. Priscilla was busy fixing up her new apartment in earth tones and rich textures, using the antiques that she loved and Elvis hated, and Elvis was busy with his personal appearances. Sometimes they seemed so friendly that many of the people around them expected that a reconciliation would eventually take place. Dee Presley commented, "I think Elvis would have gladly taken her back and tried to make the marriage work if Cilla would have gone back, but I don't think she felt she ever could go back after what happened. Elvis called her every day for a while: I know how much he had to love her and missed her, especially that first Christmas she was not at Graceland. It was so empty. They were never the same after Cilla left."

On January 8, 1973, as agreed upon, Elvis filed for divorce. (If Priscilla had brought the action, she would have had to give her address, and she and Elvis were both fearful of a kidnap attempt against Lisa.) He had begun to spend most of his time with new girlfriend, Linda Thompson, and yet it was obvious that he still hadn't gotten over the loss of Priscilla. He added a new song to his nightclub act, "You Gave Me a Mountain This Time," written by Marty Robbins. It's a sad ballad sung by a man whose wife has left him, taking away his "one ray of sunshine" and leaving him a mountain of grief that he fears he will never be able to climb. He also liked to sing a song written by Red West, "Separate Ways," which seemed to reveal his hurt feelings after the breakup. In an interview he said sentimentally, "I always feel that Priscilla is my wife. That is a great heartbreak I have never fully recovered from."

Those around him were concerned by the strength and duration of his reaction. According to T. G. Sheppard, now a singer in his own right but then a publicist with Elvis's record label, Elvis saw the failure of his marriage as a turning point in his life: "Seemed like life became more difficult. It didn't flow like it did before." Sheppard said that Elvis frequently talked to his intimates about how wonderful a happy marriage could be. "He talked about his marriage a lot to my wife and myself. He'd say, 'I don't want you two to ever split up.' And his voice would crack sometimes. I could see he was hurtin'."

His secretary remembers, "He tried to be cheerful during those days and occasionally he stopped in the office to talk. Now and then he warned us to watch out, because he was a swinging bachelor again. But he didn't fool us. He was terribly hurt."

One of the Memphis Mafia put it more strongly: "It was as if he took the third strike. His twin brother died at birth—that was strike one. Then his mama died—that was strike two. Number three was Priscilla divorcing him."

Elvis's stepmother thought she saw the depth of his pain. "He had it all within the palm of his hand. He had a beautiful wife and a beautiful little daughter that he couldn't be with, and I think that hurt him tremendously; he couldn't spend more time with her even though she was his life. Elvis Presley wasn't going to change for any woman; he had to be accepted the way he was. You know, in his heart, Elvis was a man capable of great emotions and a very deep love. He knew that all of those girls didn't mean a thing. I believe that he would have given just about anything to make just one woman happy—without needing to prove anything to anyone."

Red West made the definitive statement on the subject several years later. "There is no doubt that his ego was very badly hurt. It happened right before our eyes. We knew it was going on when he didn't even know. Now, I don't blame her for leaving Elvis. She had a life that no normal woman could put up with. But I do know he loved that woman. Even today he would never have a word said against her. He always told me, 'I will always have a love for Priscilla.' In fact, deep down, I believe that Priscilla was one of only two people he *ever* really did love in his whole life. He didn't love us. We thought he did. But he did love that woman Priscilla."

Chapter 11

☆ ☆ ☆

The Divorce Settlement

In the fall of 1972, Elvis and Priscilla Presley discussed an official separation agreement. Elvis said he was willing to give Priscilla anything she wanted. Priscilla said she was willing to trust Elvis to make a fair settlement. This seemed to be the perfect basis for a friendly settlement, but as events were to show, friendliness was not enough. A little knowledge would have helped. Both Priscilla and Elvis were sadly ignorant about the Presley financial affairs.

Priscilla doesn't try to disguise the fact that she was very naive about money at that time. She had lived with Elvis since she was sixteen. All she knew about managing money was how to sign her name to a credit-card slip. Her needs were provided for before she even had to ask: houses, cars, jewels, furs, horses, a ranch, a fantasy wardrobe. She had no idea of how much this bounty cost and therefore no idea of how much it was going to take for her to live in the future.

At the request of Elvis's lawyers she drew up a list of her projected expenses. She concluded that she could live on $1,000 a month, plus $500 child support for Lisa Marie. In addition to the alimony she was to receive one lump sum, and she asked Elvis to name the figure. He came up with $100,000, which probably sounded like a generous sum to him because he saw the settlement as just one more in a long line of gifts to his wife. He had always loved to give her things—in fact, he loved to give to everyone and sometimes gave valuable jewelry and cars to total strangers. He saw the settlement in this context, rather than as a sharing of his estate... about which he, himself, really knew very little. The Colonel and his father handled all the financial affairs, and Elvis simply spent whatever he wanted to, as long as his daddy agreed.

Considering what Elvis was worth and how much he was earning, Priscilla's settlement was definitely unfair. But neither Elvis nor Priscilla realized it at the time. And no one pointed it out to them. Elvis's lawyers and advisers thought they were acting in his best interests by giving Priscilla the smallest amount possible. And Priscilla, trusting Elvis despite their differences, was being advised by Elvis's lawyer and even coached by him about what to say to the lawyer who would represent her, a lawyer whom he had selected.

It didn't take Priscilla long to learn that she had hopelessly underestimated her financial needs. She couldn't begin to live on $1,000 a month, nor was there any need for her to. Things became especially difficult after Vernon Presley discovered that she was still using her old charge accounts and closed them all out in his desire to protect Elvis.

When Priscilla revised her estimate of her costs of living, it looked like this:

Rent	$700
Property insurance and taxes	$100
Maintenance of residence	$500
Food and household supplies	$1,000
Utilities	$150
Telephone	$400
Laundry and cleaning	$300
Clothing	$2,500
Medical	$200
Insurance	$300
Child care	$500
School	$300
Entertainment	$500
Incidentals	$1,500
Transportation	$1,000
Auto expenses	$500
Installment payments	$1,350
	$11,800

In other words, her "incidentals" were now as large as she had previously estimated her entire monthly budget to be. She had learned a lot about the reality of existence after she left the fantasy world of Graceland.

By the time Priscilla grasped the magnitude of her mistake, it was too late, under California law, to ask for a change on the simple grounds of error. In order to revise the settlement, she had to make an allegation of fraud.

Attorney Arthur Toll, of the California law firm of Tankel, Toll and Leavitt, filed a petition on Priscilla's behalf on May 29, 1973. The petition charged that Priscilla Presley had been the victim of "extrinsic fraud." In her deposition Priscilla said she was told at the time that the settlement was fair. She explained why she believed it: "Since I was sixteen years old, I have been living with my husband's family, and during that time I developed trust and confidence in my husband, his father, and other persons associated with them." This trust led her to an unquestioning acceptance of the settlement she was offered. Her petition told the whole story of how the settlement was negotiated and how she was advised by Elvis's lawyer. She said she didn't realize at the time that the settlement was unfair, because she knew nothing about Elvis's business affairs. Even when she had signed their joint tax return, she didn't look at the figures but simply put her name where she was told to.

Elvis's advisers responded by hiring a new lawyer and trying to destroy Priscilla's case. The lawyer attempted to show that she knew all along that Elvis was a rich man and that she had participated in buying and furnishing several of his houses, so she ought to have been aware of the amount of money he was spending. That might have been true in an ordinary household but not in Elvis Presley's, for the people around him all seem to agree that even he didn't really know how much he was spending. The truth of the matter was that Elvis himself probably didn't look at his tax return before he signed it. In the same way that Priscilla trusted Elvis, Elvis trusted his daddy, and neither husband nor wife knew about the reality of their income or expenditures. Whenever Vernon Presley worried out loud to his son about his ruinous extravagance, Elvis just smiled and told him not to worry: he would just go out and make another movie, another record, or arrange another Vegas appearance. The money was out there, and all he had to do was agree to accept it. That was all Elvis knew about balancing a budget—and in truth, for all of his life, it proved to be enough.

Priscilla's legal move put an additional strain on her already shaky relationship with Elvis. Although he was always a generous man, he didn't like the implication that he had cheated her. And he was uneasy about her new demands. Her lawyer began pressing to obtain information about the extent of his income and net worth, and that got everyone around Graceland all upset. According to Jerry Hopkins, "The image projected publicly was that everything was friendly, and during this period it was not, although Elvis told friends repeatedly that Priscilla could have anything she wanted. The lawyers, apparently, had negotiated with Elvis's 'best interests' in mind but without Elvis's full knowledge of what they were doing." Secretary Becky Yancey makes the point that throughout this period Elvis continued to give Priscilla gifts of clothes and jewelry and to pay her bills without question.

In the end, a new settlement was reached that seemed fair to everyone. Priscilla got $2 million, with half to be paid at the time of the settlement and the other half in monthly installments of $6,000. In addition, there was $6,000 a month alimony for one year (this figure comes from the secretary who wrote out the checks) and $4,000 a month child support for Lisa Marie. Priscilla also got half the proceeds of the sale of their Los Angeles house (it was valued at about $500,000) and 5 percent of the stock in two of Elvis's music publishing companies. The two of them would share custody of their daughter, but Lisa Marie would live with Priscilla.

The settlement seems to have restored their affection for one another. Priscilla worried about Elvis's health, and he worried about her happiness. She came to see him perform in Vegas, and he introduced her to the audience. "We are the best of friends and always have been," proclaimed Elvis. "Our divorce came about not because of another man but because of circumstances involving my career. . . . I don't think it was fair on Priscilla, with me gone so often and traveling so much."

On October 11 of that year Elvis and Priscilla were officially divorced in a court in Santa Monica. Pictures showed them emerging from the courtroom together, holding hands and parting with a kiss. Priscilla later revealed that Elvis whispered as he left, "For always and ever." Elvis looked terrible. He was much heavier; his face was swollen and his eyes puffy. Priscilla said that even his hands were swollen, and he was perspiring heavily. The strain of his bizarre life-style, his heavy use of drugs, and his sadness over the end of his marriage were all beginning to take their toll. Six days later he checked into a hospital, ostensibly to treat "recurring pneumonia" but actually to detoxify from some of the drugs he was taking, especially Demerol. He stayed there nearly three weeks, and the day he left, he promptly got stoned again.

He returned to Graceland and tried to carry on. He had his daughter with him that Christmas, and his girlfriend, Linda Thompson, hung her Christmas stocking where Priscilla's used to go. But insiders say that most of his presents remained unopened under the tree for weeks. He gave his usual big New Year's Eve party but stayed upstairs in his bedroom most of the night, appearing for no more than fifteen minutes.

Priscilla, on the other hand, looked better than she had in years. She had stopped dyeing her hair the deep artificial black that Elvis liked and allowed it to go back to its natural light brown. No longer teased and stiff, it fell down to frame her small face. Without the heavy eye makeup that Elvis had also insisted on, the real beauty of her features was even more evident. As always, she was impeccably dressed. On that particular occasion she had chosen a sort of sophisticated hippie look with a patchwork leather coat and a few big pieces of handmade jewelry.

The pictures tell the story. Most of the rest of Elvis's short life would be downhill. His use of drugs would increase, as would his isolation from reality. Even the thrill of a live performance would no longer lift him out of his depression.

As for Priscilla, she embarked on the exciting but scary process of finding herself.

Chapter 12

After the Divorce

Priscilla Presley badly wanted her freedom. She had given up the security of her marriage, the financial cushion of her unlimited checking account, and the protection of a twenty-four-hour-a-day entourage ready to jump at the boss's wife's slightest whim.

Now she had what she wanted. She knew it was going to be a difficult period. But she explained, "Even though I've always been sheltered and have sheltered myself, I also have to know about life, to be aware, to know what's going on. I've never wanted to be around only people who are locked in a prestigious life-style because that's not real. I want to be in there with people who are struggling to do what they care about."

One of the first questions Priscilla had to answer was what *she* cared about. For so many years her interests and activities had all revolved around Elvis. Now it was time to find out about herself.

One thing she knew was important to her

was fashion. When Priscilla first went to live with Elvis, he picked out all her clothes and dictated the way he wanted her to dress. But as the years passed, Priscilla became more and more inclined to dress for herself... and there is no question that her own taste was much better. Elvis's preference for dyed black hair, heavy makeup, and flashy clothes tended to make Priscilla look like a lady of the evening rather than a respectable wife and mother. Not only were the clothes he picked out for her in bad taste, but also they were not becoming to her petite size and classically beautiful features.

But with the money Priscilla had to spend on clothes and the amount of time she had to think about them during those years when she saw so little of Elvis, she had naturally begun to learn how to dress well and in a variety of styles. As a writer for *US* magazine put it, "One day she's all Calvin Klein chic, the next she's an ethnic gypsy in braids."

So it seemed natural for her to think of a career that would be involved with fashion. In 1973, she decided to go into partnership with a friend, Olivia Bis, and open a boutique in stylish Beverly Hills. Olivia was a professional designer who had in the past made dresses for Priscilla from Priscilla's own sketches. Priscilla liked to wear original creations—it was one way she could hold her own when she went out with Elvis in his outlandish costumes. Priscilla and Olivia decided to call the shop Bis & Beau, and they also decided that they would create some original designs of their own to sell in the shop. Priscilla recalls "sitting in a fabric showroom for the first time—swamped by rolls and rolls of yardage, having to figure out costs and quantity and being floored by all the new responsibility."

According to Becky Yancy, the boutique was one of the reasons why Priscilla discovered that her original settlement with Elvis was woefully inadequate. Becky explained, "She was excited about the boutique when she talked with me, but she admitted that she was shocked at the cost of launching the new business. 'It's costing more than I thought it would, Becky,' she said. 'I'm running short of money.'" In addition to the costs of setting up and stocking the shop itself, there were the costs of creating and manufacturing their original designs, and, of course, also the cost of promoting the shop to fashionable Californians. A boutique owner must keep in touch with "the beautiful people," to let them know about the store and the clothes it stocks, and, of course, the owner must be well dressed while doing it.

Elvis was very supportive of Priscilla's plans. And when the time for the shop's opening was near, he called a friend who was director of publicity at the Tropicana Hotel and asked him to help get media attention for the event. He respected Priscilla's desire to have a success of her own.

Bis & Beau *was* a commercial success. Thanks to Priscilla's sense of style and her contacts with celebrities, her clothes were sold to a number of rich and famous women. The list included Cher, Lana Turner, Natalie Wood, Suzanne Pleshette, Cybill Shepherd, Julie Christie, Eva Gabor, Linda Blair, and Twiggy: a diverse clientele. Some years later Priscilla gave an interview in which she spoke of this boutique-owning period of her life somewhat dismissively. "It was mostly something to do after my divorce," she explained. "But I was there every day, and it was work." No doubt that those facts alone made it a good experience for her at the time.

Like most other recently divorced people, Priscilla found that it took her a while to adjust to her new life. One of the casualties of the adjustment was her relationship with Mike Stone. As so often happens, the relationship that catalyzed the divorce did not survive it by long. The happiness that Priscilla had found with a man who was able to give her a fair share of his time and attention, and willing to make their relationship one of the most important aspects of his own life, faded away. She then had a brief affair with a hairdresser . . . and no subsequent serious relationship until 1978. Perhaps she realized instinctively that her first priority was to find herself and establish her own needs and desires. Only then could she choose a partner to share her life with.

Meanwhile Elvis remained an important figure in her world. For Christmas that first year they were divorced, he gave her a Jaguar worth $10,000. Becky Yancey says he also gave her an expensive sapphire bracelet a few months later. They were usually in close touch. Elvis talked to Priscilla about the new women in his life, and she talked to him about her concern for his health. All that she heard on that score was alarming. She urged him to take care of himself, and at least once she tried to use her influence to get him the help he obviously needed.

John O'Grady, a California detective who was also a member of Elvis's entourage, remembers that he and Elvis's lawyer Ed Hookstratton (the same man who had handled the Presley divorce) asked Priscilla's cooperation with one such plan in the summer of 1976. "I called Ed Hookstratton and I told him I gave Elvis one year to live unless we got him in a hospital. We made quiet arrangements for a hospital in San Diego, the Scripps Clinic, which is known for drying out rich drunks and rich drug cases. He was going to remain there for three or four months and then we were going to take him to a private estate in Hawaii on Maui, for the rest of the year, to recuperate. I had dinner with Priscilla and her sister Michelle, and we presented the whole program. Priscilla agreed, and she took it to Elvis and he rejected it. She flew to Memphis and he said he could handle it, he didn't need outside help."

Aside from their emotional bond, Elvis and Priscilla remained connected by their shared love for their daughter Lisa Marie. Elvis saw his ex-wife and daughter fairly frequently in California, and on several occasions Priscilla went back to Graceland with Lisa Marie for a visit. When the three of them were together, the atmosphere seems to have been happy. Priscilla remembers, "It was like we were never divorced. Elvis and I still hugged each other, still had love. We would say, 'Mommy said this' and 'Daddy said that.' That helped Lisa to feel stable. There was never any arguing or bitterness."

Priscilla made it easy for Elvis to see his daughter. David Stanley recalls, "He'd be just sitting there and up and get the urge to talk to her and get her on the phone, or if he was in Vegas, he just might send me to L.A. to go bring her out for a little visit. When Elvis wanted to see Lisa, he could see her anytime he wanted, unless Lisa had something very important to do."

But Priscilla reveals that there was some continuing conflict about raising Lisa. A devoted and conscientious mother, she was well aware of the problems that might come to her daughter because of Elvis's fame. She didn't want to make matters any more complicated by spoiling Lisa or by giving her everything on a silver platter. But that, of course, was exactly what Elvis liked to do for everyone he cared about...and his daughter was no exception.

When Lisa went to visit her father, Priscilla would phone regularly to check that Elvis was keeping the child on some sort of regular schedule. She recalls ruefully the time Lisa was in Vegas with her father and Priscilla called at one in the morning to talk to Elvis. He told her Lisa had gone to bed and was asleep, but a few minutes later his Aunt Delta came on the line to complain that Lisa wouldn't take her bath and go to bed. Caught in his deception, Elvis said pleadingly, "Oh, let her stay up." He didn't want her to miss a minute of the fun. Priscilla also laughingly tells the story of the tooth fairy. "When one of Lisa's baby teeth fell out here, the tooth fairy left her fifty cents. Another tooth fell out when she was with her father in Las Vegas, and *that* tooth fairy left her five dollars. When I told Elvis that fifty cents would be more in line, he laughed. He knew I was not criticizing him: how would Elvis Presley know the going rate for a tooth?"

Another example of Elvis's questionable judgment about what was suitable for a child was his gift to Lisa when she was just eight years old of a diamond ring and a fur coat. Dee Presley recalled how Priscilla handled that one. "Priscilla has always been a good mother. She had to keep Lisa Marie's feet on the ground or her father would have spoiled her to death. I remember when Lisa Marie was about eight and Elvis bought her diamond earrings and a fur coat. Priscilla said they were lovely and explained to her that they would be put away until she was older. Elvis was so caught up in himself, he didn't think too much about bringing up Lisa. It was all up to Priscilla."

Priscilla also remembers that occasion and comments tactfully, "He just needed to be enlightened a little bit." Talking about the episode made her remember how Elvis used to tease her by saying, "You know, you're no fun to give presents to, because you could live in a shack and be happy." In Priscilla's eyes material possessions are nice to have, but they are not the most important things in the world. "I think I've always had my feet on the ground and that's why I've been able to survive. I've always, deep inside, known that happiness is really peace of mind. I stress that to my daughter all the time. When I say I want to give her the best, I don't mean the best things, but the best in understanding and communication, and in hearing what she has to say. It's not that I put down having things. It can be wonderful, it gives you freedom. I just feel that unless you have peace of mind to go along with it, it means nothing."

Priscilla kept searching for her own peace of mind. "I wasn't fulfilled," she explains. "I felt something was missing." She sold her interest in the boutique in 1976, and she did some extensive traveling, all by herself, for a while. She says, "I love roughing it. I love traveling, riding the rapids, scuba diving—I go for the daring stuff. I want to try skydiving but I haven't got the nerve yet. I want to know how things work; I want to taste the *thrill* of things."

Oddly enough she found that her thoughts kept returning to the possibility of a career as an actress. It was unexpected, because she had always been very shy in public. In her autobiography she tells of an early occasion when her shyness caused her trouble. It was back in Austin, Texas, when she was elected queen of her junior high school. She hadn't expected to win the election, and she hadn't prepared anything to say. On the stage she was just dying of shyness. The fact that her father was watching her with a disappointed expression on his face didn't make matters any better, and when she finally opened her mouth to speak, all she could do was apologize to the audience.

Perhaps it was that very shyness that made her interested in the challenge of acting. Or maybe, like many shy people before her, she found that pretending to be another person helped her deal with the shyness and conquer it. Whatever the reason, she began to take acting lessons. By the summer of 1977, it looked as if she might be ready to embark on a new career.

But she was distracted by her worry about her ex-husband. When she spoke to him on the telephone, he sounded very low. When she'd asked him anxiously if he was all right, he would answer that he was just tired... she was not to worry. She knew he'd been in and out of the hospital, and the last time she'd seen him, in April of that year, he had looked dreadful. Still, there were times when he seemed like the old Elvis. Priscilla likes to remember one of their last telephone conversations. They were discussing his new relationship with Ginger Alden, and she asked him if he thought he could ever really live with just one woman.

"Yes," he answered. "Now more than ever. I know I've done some stupid things, but the stupidest was not realizing what I had until I lost it. I want my family back." I wondered if there was some way we could make it work.

"Maybe it was just too early in life for us, Sattnin," I said. "Maybe one day there will be a time for us."

"Yeah," Elvis laughed. "When I'm seventy and you're sixty. We'll both be so old we'll look really silly, racing around in golf carts."

But the time for a reconciliation between Elvis and Priscilla never came.

Chapter 13

☆ ☆ ☆

The Death of Elvis

Priscilla Presley remembers all too clearly what it was like the day Elvis died.

She was meeting her sister Michelle for lunch, and when she arrived, Michelle was standing on the street corner with a concerned look on her face. She told Priscilla she'd heard from their father that Joe Esposito was trying to reach her from Memphis. She rushed back home to be near the telephone, and it rang almost the instant she walked in the door. Joe told her the news. They both began to cry.

After that first wave of sorrow her next concern was for her daughter, who happened to be visiting at Graceland; everyone hoped that seeing Lisa Marie would cheer Elvis up. How was Lisa taking the terrible event? Joe reassured her that Lisa was all right and that she was with Elvis's grandmother. Then he told Priscilla that he'd sent Elvis's private plane to get her right away. He knew she'd want to arrive at Graceland as soon as possible.

Elvis's death was perhaps not really a surprise to those who were close to him, since the deterioration in his spirits and his health had been plain for them to see. But it was an overwhelming sorrow to all the people whose lives were so intertwined with his. Vernon Presley was nearly prostrate with grief, and the entourage of the Memphis Mafia seemed frozen by the shock. Graceland became the center of all the mourning.

As with most of the important events of Elvis's life, his death was not just a private grief but a public event. The family quickly realized that the thousands of fans who were already gathering outside the gates must somehow be included. It was decided to have Elvis lie in state in the drawing room, and fans would be allowed to pass by and pay their respects. It is estimated that the crowd numbered at least 75,000, and so many floral tributes (over 3,000) were sent that they filled the house and lined the driveway.

The press was out in full force. Geraldo Rivera was there for ABC, Charles Kuralt for CBS. The *National Enquirer* sent a team of twenty reporters, and *Rolling Stone* had journalists not only in Memphis but also in Tupelo, Mississippi, Elvis's birthplace. Correspondents as diverse as Pete Hamill and Caroline Kennedy were filing reports datelined Memphis.

Inside the house, in the family's private

quarters, Priscilla was doing her best to cope with the situation. Lisa was taking her father's death hard. She'd heard the commotion in the house when girlfriend Ginger Alden found Elvis (almost certainly already dead) lying on his bathroom floor. But Ginger had reassured ten-year-old Lisa that her daddy was going to be all right, and Lisa had played unconcernedly for several hours before the news was broken to her. David Stanley observed, "She knew that her daddy was dead, but she just couldn't figure it out. Only her mother would be able to help her do that." Priscilla knew how close Lisa felt to her father and worried about how Lisa would adjust to his loss.

Priscilla took Lisa up to Elvis's bedroom, and the two of them cried together. Says Priscilla, "I was so devastated. His death was the greatest loss I had ever experienced." Then the two people closest to Elvis picked out things they wanted to remember him by. "She picked out a golf cap and his electric razor, because they were 'close to Daddy.' I took his cane, it was so much him. He never went anywhere without it, and the scent of Elvis's hand, the cologne he wore, was on the handle."

Carefully Priscilla chose a time when she and Lisa could say their final good-bye to Elvis. It was the night before his funeral, which would, of course, be conducted in the glare of worldwide publicity. The open coffin had been moved to the living room where the funeral would be held, and the doors of Graceland had been closed to the steady parade of weeping fans. Holding Lisa's hand, Priscilla stood over Elvis and spoke to him softly. She was thankful to see that he looked peaceful at last, and she hoped that he had finally found the answers he'd been looking for. She and Lisa put on his wrist a silver bracelet that depicted a mother and child's clasped hands. She knew that the man they were telling good-bye would always be an important part of her life, and her daughter's as well.

For the funeral itself, Priscilla dressed in a very simple black dress and tied back her long hair with a neat ribbon. The living room was packed with about two hundred people—family and celebrity guests, including George Hamilton and Ann-Margret and her husband Roger Smith. Elvis's favorite gospel singers performed: Jake Hess, James Blackwood, and the Stamps. Jewish comedian Jackie Kahane delivered one eulogy; another was given by the family pastor. Then a white hearse and a procession of seventeen white limousines went to the cemetery where Elvis was interred. The next day, 50,000 fans visited his grave. After a few months his body was moved back to Graceland for greater security, and his mother's was transferred there as well. It was later revealed that Elvis's funeral had cost over $46,000.

Afterward Priscilla faced the immediate problem of what to do for Lisa. She decided to send her away to camp immediately, to get her away from the sadness of Graceland. "She was around playful kids and didn't hear the news all the time. She was still hurt, but she's very secure." There was some criticism of this move—perhaps just because there were people ready to criticize everything Elvis's widow did. Later she defended her decision, saying, "It was the best thing I could have done. Now Lisa says she didn't have time to think about her father's death and has a much healthier attitude."

Priscilla soon had to face another set of demands. Although she was not a beneficiary of Elvis's will, she was one of its executors. Her main concern was looking out for the interests of Lisa, who was Elvis's principal heir. Her own initiation into the real world when she separated from Elvis made her suspect that the estate might be in a muddle, and she was quite right. Despite the fact that Elvis had earned what some people estimate to be well over a $1 billion—perhaps even $2 billion—over the course of his career, it was not even certain that the estate was solvent.

Years after the funeral Dee Presley told a curious story to a journalist from *McCall's*, about Priscilla's out-of-character behavior

on the day of the funeral. "The funeral was
at Graceland, and it was the last day I would
ever be there. It was very rough for me. Priscilla came over to me, and I thought it was
to console me. But instead she handed me
some contracts and asked me to sign over
certain movie rights to her. It was what she
called 'business.' She had become very cal-
lous."

If Priscilla was asking Dee Presley to sign
something, it was probably because she was
already worried about the estate. Moreover,
according to Albert Goldman, Colonel Parker was, during the same period, asking
Vernon Presley to sign documents that would
insure that all his own lucrative deals continued and that he would be able to exploit
Elvis's career even after his death.

Priscilla's worries were confirmed when
the estate was probated several years after
Elvis's death. The total came to just a little
over $7 million, and that included $3 million due in royalties on the sale of records
and other items but not yet paid. Although
an earlier estimate had put the value of the
estate at about twice that amount, various
debts and obligations had reduced its total.
Among them was the nearly $500,000 mort-
gage against Graceland that Elvis had taken
out in 1977 to meet the requirements of his
divorce settlement with Priscilla.

Luckily Priscilla's business experience
with the boutique had given her some hard-

won knowledge, and she was able to analyze the situation and decide what should be done. Vernon Presley died in 1979, leaving Priscilla and her lawyers in control of the entire estate. At about the same time the IRS announced that it was valuing the estate at $25 million, and the State of Tennessee went them even better and placed a value of $31 million on Elvis's estate. They arrived at these high figures by calculating the value of royalties to come, a process that lawyers for the estate disputed. The court-appointed attorney for Lisa Marie's interests said, "I don't see how in the world they decided the estate was worth that. It doesn't seem right. Why would the estate be taxed for income that came after he died?"

While the lawyers debated, the IRS demanded over $14 million in inheritance taxes. An IRS lawyer explained, "The big thing that's holding up probate is coming to a resolution with state and federal tax authorities. Negotiations are ongoing." He added sympathetically, "Priscilla's job is to conserve as much as possible for Lisa Marie; unless we can get rid of the tax liabilities, there will be no money for her."

The Colonel and Elvis had had a system for dealing with the IRS that was very unusual for anyone earning the large amount of money Elvis did. They gave the government the complete figures on his income, and the tax men filled out the tax form and

decided how much income tax was due...
no tax shelters, no loopholes, no big deduc-
tions. But Priscilla and her lawyers were
going to fight for every penny. They had to,
or else the estate would be bankrupt.

While fighting the IRS on one side, Priscilla reluctantly decided that she would have
to fight Colonel Parker on the other. Lisa's
attorney, Blanchard Tual, conducted a year-
long investigation of Parker's financial dealings with Elvis and with the estate. Tual
presented his findings to the probate judge,
charging that the Colonel had "violated his
duty both to Elvis and to the estate" and
had charged commissions that were "excessive, imprudent... and beyond all reasonable bounds of industry standards." The
judge immediately ordered that all payments from the estate to Parker should
cease, and additionally instructed Tual to
file charges against Parker to recover money
already paid out by the estate to him. Priscilla, who had initially gone along with Vernon's request to continue doing business as
usual with the Colonel, realized that she
would have to support Tual's suit to protect
her daughter's inheritance. Later RCA Records joined the proceedings as well, hoping
to put an end to the large royalties they had
to pay the Colonel for every Elvis Presley record sold.

In 1983, a settlement among the parties
was reached without going to court. RCA

agreed to buy out Parker's interests in all Elvis recordings for a $2 million lump sum. Additionally, they paid the estate over $1 million to win an amended contract that gave them exclusive rights to all Presley recordings. They also set up royalty payments to the estate for foreign sales and record club sales. The Colonel, for his part, won a ratification that all the income he had earned before Elvis's death was his to keep. In return he gave up his ongoing involvement with the estate and sold his rights in a company he formed to merchandise Elvis's name and likeness to the estate for a reasonable figure. He agreed to turn over all the Elvis memorabilia he had in his possession and not to exploit Elvis any further without full consent of the estate. Finally he agreed not to mention Elvis in print unless the book or article was primarily about himself rather than Elvis; that move delayed, or possibly stopped, the Elvis biography the Colonel was said to be writing. The estate issued an announcement that the matters of controversy had been amicably resolved, and concluded graciously, "Colonel Parker has clearly been a major factor in the enormous success which Elvis Presley enjoyed and the Co-Executors of the Estate have asked that their gratitude be extended to the Colonel for his unique and dedicated service."

One other major problem of the estate

concerned Priscilla, and that was Graceland. At the time of Elvis's death it was valued at about $500,000, plus another $200,000 for the household furnishings. Several years later Jack Soden, the executive director of Elvis Presley Enterprises (the corporation the estate formed after Elvis's death), said that the annual upkeep on the house was the same figure, $500,000. With utility bills of nearly $1,000 a month, a huge payroll of family and former entourage to maintain and guard the place, gardeners keeping the lawns green and stable boys looking after Elvis's horses and dogs, it's easy to see how the costs mounted.

But since the estate itself was in such bad financial shape, it could not afford to keep supporting the huge cost of running Graceland. According to Jack Soden, "Out of sheer necessity, Priscilla had to think about liquidation." In the end she came up with a plan that stopped the drain on the estate and still preserved Graceland just the way Elvis left it. "It was an emotional decision for her," said Soden, "but in the spring of 1982, we opened Graceland as a museum instead. There are three executors, but Priscilla is the one with the emotional investment." He concluded, "Not many people realize what Graceland means to Priscilla."

It was Priscilla who set up the ground rules for converting Elvis's beloved home into a museum. She decreed that no money would change hands on the grounds of Graceland. Tickets are sold, and tours begin and end off the premises. She would allow neither souvenirs nor snacks to be sold at Graceland itself. And she decided to open only the grounds and the downstairs of the mansion. It took five years, and a sizable investment, to restore Graceland to all its former grandeur. "But," says Priscilla contentedly, "we put it in its original shape, the way it was when Elvis was happy."

Priscilla presided over the opening of Graceland as a museum, and it has been a great success. In the first year it was open, more than a million people flocked to tour Graceland (paying ten dollars apiece). They get to see the stables, the racquetball court, and the gravesite where Elvis and his parents are buried. Elvis's favorite horse, Rising Sun, can be glimpsed in the pasture, and his Pomeranian, Edmund, often accompanies the tours. At the house, awed fans go through the living room, dining room, pool room, trophy room, music room, TV room, and den. The tour ends with a look at his collection of motorcycles and cars, including that 1955 pink Cadillac he bought his mother when his success first began. Back across the street, fans can go through Elvis's private plane, with the double bed circled by a big safety belt, the $15,000 stereo system, and the monogrammed silver in the dining room.

For Priscilla, Elvis is still very near when she is at Graceland. She stays there whenever business takes her to the Memphis area, and the memories of Elvis come flooding back. This is where she remembers him at his best. "My happiest memories of Elvis are the times—there were few of them—when he dropped that wall, when he became the person he might have been without all the pressure. Nights when he'd come into Lisa's bedroom—he always called her 'Yeesa'—and read her nursery rhymes on the bed. And the day he bought horses for everyone at Graceland. I can still see him out there in the dirt, in his jeans and heavy coat and cowboy hat, going around, writing everybody's name on the stalls with a red marking pen—watering the horses, blanketing them. He looked so satisfied, so . . . simple."

And perhaps, alone at Graceland late at night, Priscilla also thinks of what might have been. In the last months of his life Elvis often called Priscilla from Graceland, and they'd talk about what they were doing and how they felt. He listened with interest as Priscilla talked about her new life and the things she was learning. "Cilla," he'd say, "go do what you have to do now. Go see the world. But when you're forty and I'm fifty, we'll be back together. You'll see."

And how did Priscilla feel about the hope

that they might eventually get back together? "I guess I never thought it was out
of the question. We were both such roman-
tics. Sometimes I think if I knew then what
I know now—that only when you're a person in your own right can you help another
person be happy—I could have made our
marriage work." She adds sadly, "But there
was no way I could have become my own
person inside that marriage."

And then death intervened, and the
chances of reconciliation were gone forever.

Chapter 14

☆ ☆ ☆

Building a Career

The death of Elvis was an emotional blow that took Priscilla a long time to recover from. She had lost a friend and confidant, a mentor and teacher. If he was no longer her lover at the time of his death, he was certainly still a man who loved her, as she did him. And, of course, he was also the father of her child.

After August 16, 1977, Priscilla was truly on her own, without Elvis in the background for emotional support and protection. She remembers that fall, when she and Lisa returned to Los Angeles, how her daughter "suddenly realized the enormousness of her loss. When it hit her that she'd never see her daddy again, that she couldn't even talk to him on the phone, she wept and said, 'Mommy, what's going to happen to us?'" Priscilla admits that at that particular moment she had no idea. But she pulled herself together and told Lisa firmly, "Well, we are going to live our lives and help each other out. It's just you and me, kid. . . ."

She was very concerned about being a good mother to Lisa. "I knew Lisa could never lead a truly normal life, but I hoped she could get her values straight." That meant understanding that the glamour of life in Beverly Hills was not reality. "Kids used to come to the house with Gucci bags and diamond earrings. I told Lisa to cool it with them because they're living in a bubble." She wanted Lisa to have the security of knowing that she was liked for herself rather than for her name or future inheritance. She taught her daughter to be wary: "I've raised her to be very cautious. I tell her not to jump into anything, to always check things out and keep her sense of humor—which she does. I've taught her to always remember that things in life are only temporary. Believe me, I could go on about *that*!"

Priscilla knew that she had to be strong for Lisa's sake. Perhaps the best thing she could do, as a role model for Lisa, was to show her that life could go on, that new satisfactions could be developed to take the place of lost happiness. For her daughter's sake as well as her own, Priscilla decided that she needed to get on with her career plans. "There's a time to hide and a time to come out. My time to come out has arrived."

She signed with the William Morris talent

agency, continued her acting lessons, and began looking for work as an actress. It was a tough decision, but she was determined to try. "I didn't want to look back some day and wish I had tried for that career while I had the chance." In an interview for *McCall's* in early 1979, she said, "I'm finally starting an acting career—or hoping to, anyway. I'm going for readings and auditions. I took acting lessons for a while, and I was going to guest-star on a Tony Orlando TV special until it got turned into a one-man show, and then ... I kind of backed away from the idea of 'going public.' I thought I'd just try to do commercials, which are safe. I'd be anonymous, just pitching a product. See, it has taken me so long to establish a normal private life that I didn't want to risk letting it go."

There was also the problem of her shyness to be faced. "I've always been very shy," Priscilla confessed. "But I'm becoming more at ease with audiences, because I'm realizing that others are often more nervous than I am. Learning that we're all basically the same has been great for my growing process."

There was another risk she faced in going out to look for work as an actress, and that was the cynicism of people who believed that she was just trying to trade on the Presley name after Elvis's death. Priscilla recalls, "The first six months of going out on interviews and to different companies, I met a lot of people and I saw the negativity that was there. I could feel the vibes. I could feel people thinking: what does she want? or who does she think she is? or she's just cashing in on this or cashing in on that. That wasn't the case at all. I wanted to work."

One of her first jobs was as model and spokeswoman for Wella hair-care products. "People think I was just offered it," Priscilla said. She added wistfully, "I wish it were that easy." She wanted to do the Wella commercials because she liked the family-owned company and believed in the products. "My hair turned green at one point from the chlorine in our swimming pool and I went through three days of changing it back to blonde. I used all the Wella products on it and I must say they really work." She commented about her commercial work: "I believe in what I'm doing now. I'm not looking for fame, fortune and stardom. I just like feeling as though I'm doing something constructive." She was offered the role of one of Charlie's Angels but turned it down because she didn't like the program. She comments, "A lot of television is a shallow look at what it's not like. I wanted to do something that was good, rewarding, beneficial and educational—and something that meant growth for me."

Early in 1980, she found the vehicle she was looking for. It was a new hour-long television show that would debut in August, *Those Amazing Animals.* The program was developed by the producers of *That's Incredible.* The host of the show, who got top billing, was Burgess Meredith. Priscilla Presley was co-host, along with country singer Jim Stafford. It was a program aimed straight at the heart of middle America, airing on Sunday night at 7 P.M. and featuring live animals, film clips of animals in action, and some human guests, such as Jacques Cousteau.

Priscilla thought the show was ideal. She had always loved animals and was the enthusiastic owner of two dogs and three cats at that time, as well as an admirer of horses and an enthusiast of the beauties of nature. "Animals," she explained, "have no ulterior motives, and once they love you, they're always there." A reporter from *US* magazine who interviewed her at the time the show was first on the air found herself getting an earful of animal lore. "Did you know there's a queen termite in Africa that lays ten thousand eggs a day for fifteen years? Do you know tarantulas have no skeletons, so if you drop them, they break right in half? Roaches? I hate them. I haven't found any use for *them*!"

Another thing she liked about the show was that it had some educational value. It was a show she would be glad to let her child watch, as opposed to most of what was on television, which she felt was "an insult to her intelligence. Here's this medium that reaches into every single home, and it does nothing to benefit our youth!"

The executive producer of the show, Merrill Grant, is quick to deny that he hired Priscilla for the value of her famous last name. He said he had seen her on talk shows and knew that she loved animals. He commented, "While her last name is not a marquee liability, it's not enough to get her signed for a prime-time television show. In this town she's considered to be an attractive, intelligent personality who can handle herself in show-business terms. We wanted her for all of those things...."

Those Amazing Animals got mixed reviews. Robert MacKenzie, writing in *TV Guide*, thought that the show suffered from having too many short segments that were thematically unrelated. He also objected to the focus on the unusual rather than the ordinary in nature. As he put it, "By the end of the season *Those Amazing Animals* should have whipped through most of the major species and found every fiddling pig and tap-dancing dog in captivity." Other reviewers lauded the fact that the show was decent family entertainment, and a lot of animal lovers stayed tuned. The show did respectably well for a season.

The experience of doing a weekly television show was good for Priscilla's career, although the value of the exposure was limited. She was overshadowed by host Burgess Meredith and, most of all, by the amazing animals who were the real stars of the show. She understood at the time she signed up to do the show that it would not make her a superstar. "I don't care about being a superstar," she explained, "but I feel I have something to give and to share, and if I can do that and maintain my values . . . well, I can."

But at least the show gave her a credential, that important first step in getting more and better acting assignments. She was determined to continue with her show-business career even though she understood its risks better than most people. She had watched what happened to Elvis as he struggled to deal with his phenomenal success. "I would just take it all in and learn from how people acted. I saw the phoniness, the bullshit, that was going on. I would sit back and think, 'My God, I don't ever want to be like that.'" Her firsthand observation of the way people tried to exploit Elvis made her very protective of herself. "You can be hurt in this business, and more than anything, I don't want to be hurt. With my background, making the most basic decisions gets difficult. Just knowing who to trust—being selective about people without being cynical—is probably the hardest thing."

One good aspect of Priscilla's life at this

time was that she had found a man she could
trust. He was an actor and model named
Michael Edwards, whom she met in early
1978. Michael was an attractive man, about
Priscilla's age, who was not dominated by
his career ambitions. His goal in life was "to
enjoy," and he helped Priscilla learn to do
just that. He didn't impose his taste or his
views on her, but he encouraged her to discover what her own were. Priscilla commented happily, "I need an equal, not a father
figure. I need a relationship with a man I
can grow with." She found that relationship
with Michael. Within months of their meeting, the couple began to live together.

They wanted to share everything. "We
don't have any egos about who does what,"
said Priscilla. "I thought I was a great cook
until Michael came along. It was very em-
barrassing—he turned out to be a gourmet
cook while I was still defrosting frozen food!
But he taught me what he knew, and now
we take turns." Thrifty Priscilla added, "Either way, it's better eating at home than paying a hundred dollars for a mediocre meal
out. The atmosphere's much better, the
wine's much better, plus you have the whole
family there." They also shared a love of
travel, and one of their happiest times was
a 1979 trip to Samoa. "We were literally living in sarongs and washing our fish and
vegetables in the ocean," Priscilla told Andy

Warhol for *Interview*. "We got totally immersed in the culture. . . . Everybody we saw wanted us to take their picture."

Yet Priscilla is always careful not to compare her new love with her old. "I've never compared Elvis to anyone or him to them. Everyone has their good points and bad points." And however fond Priscilla was of Michael, she refused to consider a second marriage. "I don't need marriage to feel whole, get security, or be more a woman. Those are inner qualities you can only give yourself. I don't believe in the romantic notion that once you're married, life becomes great and wonderful. Believe me, it wasn't like that at all! That piece of paper never stopped any arguments. As long as you're secure with each other, then you're fine."

Michael encouraged her to go on pursuing her dream of success as an actress. Together they enrolled in the acting class of Milton Katselas; former students included Tom Selleck and Cheryl Ladd. Katselas emphasized discipline and responsibility: an actor should appear on the set on time with all lines fully memorized. He combined this strictness with the upbeat you-can-win-if-you-think-you-can approach of scientology, and Priscilla found that it worked for her. (She even enrolled Lisa one year in a school run by a group of scientologists.)

With Michael's support Priscilla was ready for new career challenges: "To do something like this," she reflected, "you need good people around you and a good family behind you." That's what gave her the confidence to accept a role in a three-hour made-for-TV movie that would also be shown as a feature film in theaters outside the U.S. The movie was originally titled *Comeback* but was eventually aired by NBC under the name *Love Is Forever*. It starred Michael Landon and co-starred Priscilla and Moira Chen.

The producer-director was Englishman Hall Bartlett, and he was asked the inevitable question of whether he hired Priscilla for the value of her name. "Absolutely not," he replied. "In fact, I assured her that in no way would we exploit that. No, I chose her because she can look at once wary and vulnerable. She has an interesting quality."

The film was based on a true story of a love affair between an Australian journalist in Laos and a beautiful Laotian woman. They planned to be married, but then he was expelled from the country by the Pathet Lao, on the charge that he was a spy. He spent weeks learning to use scuba equipment and practicing his plan to go back to Laos to get his fiancée. The rescue mission, in which he swam across the Mekong River, where she was waiting in her scuba gear, and then swam back with her on the bottom of the river with the police shooting wildly into the water, proved to be successful, and the couple lived happily ever after.

Priscilla's part in the movie was that of the scuba teacher. Michael Edwards, who had once been a marine diving instructor, went along with Priscilla on location in Thailand and the Bahamas and taught her how to do the underwater scenes. "The very first time," Priscilla told a reporter, "I sat on the edge of the board, crying with fear. Finally, I rocked back and he pushed me in." Director Bartlett had nothing but praise for Priscilla's effort. "The moment she'd committed to the film, she began learning how to dive and swim under water. That impressed me a lot. Here's a woman many people think must be utterly spoiled, getting up at five A.M. to train for a role." Al Giddings, who directed all the underwater scenes, was also impressed. "She's done in three or four days what Jacqueline Bisset took three or four weeks to do in *The Deep.* But she was not only gutsy; she swims with the natural grace of a dolphin."

One of the scenes called for Priscilla and Michael Landon to swim unconcernedly while sharks patrolled nearby. Landon called for a stunt double, but Priscilla decided to do the scene herself. "I worked so hard to get it right," she explained later. "I didn't want to let it go. After all the anguish and tears, I wasn't going to give it up to someone else." Bartlett was more impressed than ever. "She was doggedly determined to do everything herself. We'd hired an experienced double, but she never once went in the water. Priscilla did it all."

Swimming with sharks was probably the easiest part of making this movie. There was a struggle for power going on between the star and the director, and the atmosphere on the set was often downright unpleasant. As Priscilla put it tactfully, "It wasn't a happy environment." Stories made their way into print about how the star shot his own scenes without even bothering to have the director present. Landon was determined to make the film as quickly as possible and go home. His co-star said, "I thought feature film work would be relaxed, that I'd have time to get comfortable before the cameras, would be able to polish each line. Whoever dreamed Landon was a one- or two-take actor? One time I thought we were just rehearsing, and before I even had a chance to realize the cameras were rolling, he said, 'Okay, that's it,' and he was gone." Michael Landon totally downplayed Priscilla's contribution to the film. He told a reporter from *People* that in their joint sequences, "It was just, 'Hello, how are you?' and then you go swimming."

Priscilla herself kept a stiff upper lip about the way Michael Landon treated her, but Hall Bartlett was much less reticent. He told the press, "Michael was especially mean to Priscilla Presley. This was her first major acting role and she was terribly nervous and insecure. Landon made fun of her frequent fixing of her hair, shouting over and over again, 'It's *Charlie's Angels* time.'"

Priscilla later remarked softly, "I did fiddle with my hair a lot, but so would any woman in a climate with a ninety-five percent humidity that makes you look like a mop—and in ten minutes."

Love Is Forever was shown in April 1983. Reviews were generally favorable, although Landon came in for more than his share of criticism for his trouble in immersing himself in another character. Unfortunately many of the reviews didn't even mention Priscilla or any of the other co-stars. Once again, she had a credit but no significant advancement for her career. At that time, what made her feel best about the whole project was that she had mastered the skill of scuba diving and made her underwater scenes look convincing—and that she had survived the problems on the set and lived to tell the tale. "I'm willing to challenge the world now," she said enthusiastically at the time, and then added cryptically, "This movie has given me *such* experience."

Priscilla would soon find out that *Love Is Forever* had given her something else as well. For watching the TV movie at home that night was Philip Capice, the executive producer of *Dallas*.

Chapter 15

Stardom on *Dallas*

Not long after *Love Is Forever* had aired on NBC, Priscilla Presley's agent began making the rounds of producers, talking up his client. Recognition of the name was instant, but often that was as far as things went. Priscilla understood the situation. "They think they know all about me from what they've read, that I'm some sort of dilettante. They invite me just because of curiosity, and that's it. The doors open because I'm Priscilla Presley and then they close even faster."

But one door that didn't close all the way was that of Lorimar Productions, the company that created *Dallas*. "When my agent submitted my name to Lorimar, they said they weren't interested. I had a tape made of some of the best things I've done and he offered to send it over. Another no. So he brought it over anyway and said, 'Don't you think she at least deserves an interview?'"

Philip Capice, the executive producer of the show, looked at Priscilla's tape. He was struck first by its shortness—"so little there, only about six minutes." There were the Wella commercials, a few minutes from *Those Amazing Animals,* a short scene from *Love Is Forever,* and a clip from a recent appearance on *The Fall Guy.* Not a very impressive collection of credits . . . but Capice says that while he was looking at the tape, he remembered seeing Priscilla in *Love Is Forever* and being impressed by how well she handled her part. "I decided to call her in," he says. "The first thing that struck me was how beautiful she is." Capice was inclined to hire her. "We were looking for someone who was extremely beautiful. You look at Priscilla's face and there aren't that many in the world who photograph like that." On the other hand, he worried about the effect of her famous name. "We wanted someone the viewers would believe in as the character. We didn't want them looking at an actress and saying, 'Oh, look, there's Elvis Presley's wife.'" After much debate Capice offered Priscilla the role of Jenna Wade. He says now, "Despite the fact that her acting experience was less than what we normally require for a major role, we haven't been at all sorry."

Along with the offer of the role came an emphasis by Capice on its rigors. The shooting schedule of a weekly hour-long program of the complexity of *Dallas* is extremely demanding. There would also be a lot of travel, because much of the show is shot on location in Texas. When he issued these warnings, Priscilla looked him right in the eye and said, "I wouldn't be here if I didn't think I could do it." Lisa was then 15 and entering high school; Priscilla was certain that she could juggle her schedule to give her teenage daughter the time she needed and still manage a prime-time series herself. She explained to a reporter, "Lisa said, 'Whatever makes you happy, Mom.' It doesn't take me away from her. I'm still wearing my mother's hat."

Her introduction to *Dallas* was a matter of sink or swim. She was hired on a Thursday; she flew to Fort Worth on Friday; and on Saturday she shot three big scenes. "I was petrified," Priscilla admits. "There were so many lines and I had never met any of the *Dallas* regulars and I wondered what they would think of me. My problem is, people know who I am but they don't know my work."

She smiles as she remembers her first scene with J. R., played by Larry Hagman. "He's so big, so intimidating," she explains. She had worked for hours to learn her lines cold, so Larry wouldn't dismiss her as an amateur. But when they played the scene, and she reeled off her letter-perfect lines, he would ask, "What's my line?" As Priscilla says, "I was so serious and he was so casual. It really threw me." Eventually it also helped her relax and concentrate on the work of acting.

One thing that worked in her favor was that she had an immediate rapport with Patrick Duffy, who played Bobby Ewing, the man to whom Jenna Wade had once been engaged and who suddenly turns up again at the cowboy café where she is working as a waitress, sparking a renewal of their love affair. Patrick had been on the show since its beginning, in 1978, and he's been through two previous Jennas—Morgan Fairchild and Francine Tacker. Producer Leonard Katzman said of Patrick, "Pat is glib, quick and funny, and if you can't keep up with him, you're in trouble." Pat recalls that he gave Priscilla no slack whatever: "I don't believe in tippytoeing around with a newcomer." But he found Priscilla to be "unaffected and not burdened with any actress paraphernalia. She simply does good clean honest work."

Of course, almost as soon as Priscilla walked on the set of the top-rated show, the rumor mills began to grind out stories... most of them completely groundless. For example, there was an early report that Priscilla was feuding with Linda Gray, whom at that time she hadn't even met. An insider related what happened when the two women finally did meet. "Linda made the first move, saying loudly, 'Okay, kid, where do you want it—here or outside?' Everyone knew what was coming next. Both Linda and Priscilla burst out laughing." Later Priscilla commented, "How could anyone have a feud with Linda? She's one of the finest persons I've ever known." In fact, Priscilla got on well with everyone. Capice termed her introduction to the cast "an instant love affair." She puts it a bit more cautiously. "They are a very tight little group but I didn't have any trouble. All my life I've always been the new girl on the block."

Priscilla very quickly found herself identifying strongly with her character, Jenna Wade. "Jenna is her own woman. She's extremely self-reliant, she has lived in Europe, and she has a child. Just like me. Except that she's a bit more sophisticated than I am. She's got a lot of integrity, she's totally honest. I like her. How could I help but identify with her?" This identification led Priscilla in her first few weeks on the set to question the script she was given. "There were a couple of things I didn't think Jenna would do," she declares. She took her complaint to producer Leonard Katzman, who comments wryly, "I don't think she knew I had also written the script." But she convinced him to make the changes she wanted.

The role of Jenna has given Priscilla the opportunity to develop as an actress. In her first season on the show Jenna was featured in a slow-developing romance with her old flame, Bobby. They had their ups and downs, many of them caused by Jenna's awareness of the fact that Bobby was still very much entangled with ex-wife Pam. Like Priscilla herself, Jenna opened a boutique and sold beautiful clothes to the fashionable women of Dallas. Eventually she agreed to marry Bobby. Meanwhile she preserved a determined silence on the question of who was the father of her daughter Charlotte, or "Charlie."

In the second season Jenna's role became considerably more dramatic. She was kidnapped by her ex-husband on the day of her wedding to Bobby, leaving him standing at the altar. Then the ex-husband was found dead in a hotel on the Mexican border and Jenna was charged with the murder. By this time Bobby had learned the reason for her disappearance and was ready to do all a Ewing could to help her. Jenna went on trial for her life; because the witness Bobby found to testify on her behalf was murdered on her way to Dallas, Jenna was convicted. Not until she had served some months of her sentence did Bobby succeed in finding new evidence that won her release. Alas, by the time she was out, he had discovered that he *was* still in love with Pam, just as Jenna suspected. After a period of indecision Bobby made up his mind to break off his relationship with Jenna and remarry Pam. But before he could tell Jenna his decision, he was killed.

This all adds up to a big acting opportunity for Priscilla Presley, and she has performed very creditably. As she heads into her third season on the show, she is one of the acknowledged stars, and audiences are waiting eagerly to see what Jenna is going to do next. The role has certainly been good for Priscilla's career.

There is, of course, the possibility that she will find herself now trapped within the role of Jenna, just as she was previously trapped within the role of Mrs. Elvis Presley. Several years ago Priscilla told a reporter breezily, "The other day at an airport a woman yelled, 'Hi, Jenna.' I loved it. It made my day. I hope I hear it for years." But that was at the beginning of her stint on the show. She may find, as have many other actors before her, that stardom on a series can be a very confining situation. Larry Hagman, for example, confesses that he doubts if he'll ever get any other roles once *Dallas* eventually goes off the air; he is so thoroughly identified with the character of J. R. Ewing that it would be difficult for audiences to accept him as any other character. If this can happen to Larry Hagman, who had already starred in one hit series before he signed up for *Dallas*, what will happen to Priscilla, whose face (minus the heavy eyeliner and beehive hairdo) was virtually unknown to the public until she took over the character of Jenna Wade?

Right now she is enjoying her success. But you can bet that this independent lady is making plans to break out of the mold of Jenna Wade before she is trapped there permanently. This is a woman who stated her ambition in these words: "You know what I want, more than anything? I want to do *everything.*"

Chapter 16

☆ ☆ ☆

Remembering Elvis

January 8, 1985, would have been Elvis Presley's fiftieth birthday. Even if he'd lived, it's unlikely that he would have celebrated the event with much joy. He certainly hadn't been happy about his fortieth. According to Joe Esposito, "Elvis's fortieth birthday was definitely a crisis for him. He didn't like the idea of being forty, and it was after that that his serious problems began. He saw himself getting older and it scared him. He didn't talk about it much—that's how we knew it bugged him tremendously."

However, to the survivors—and that included millions of fans all over the world—Elvis's birthday was a very special day: a chance to pay homage to a man of special gifts and enormous charisma. Many tributes were planned to mark the occasion.

No one really expected Priscilla Beaulieu Presley to take part in any of the public commemorations of Elvis's life. During her marriage to Elvis the entourage had protected her from reporters so that she never had to

face them. Immediately after her divorce she
did her best to stay out of the public eye and
out of the reach of the press. Even after Elvis's death she had adopted a firm policy of
simply never speaking about her life with
him. There was certainly a period when she
could have used publicity as an actress, but
she still refused to grant any interviews unless the reporter accepted the ground rule
that there would be no questions about Elvis.

The reasons for Priscilla's silence were
numerous. One of them was pride. She was
determined not to appear to trade on the
Presley name. She told Andy Warhol about
her annoyance when people accused her of
doing just that. "People ask me if I get into
a big career will I change my name; why
should I change my name? I have a daughter and it's her name too. Some people ac-
cuse me of trying to cash in on the name.
Well, that's totally untrue. If I had wanted to
cash in on the name, I would have done it
years ago. I believe I would be doing the same
thing I'm doing now regardless of my name.
... Sometimes my name works for me and
sometimes it works against me."

Another reason for her silence was the
fact that many people had virtually accused
her of killing Elvis by leaving him. Few people understood her reasons for doing so (especially since she had remained silent about

them), and nearly everyone blamed her for it. Even the mildest letters must have been hurtful. May Mann quotes one letter that she herself received about the situation; surely Priscilla must have received thousands in the same vein. "I can appreciate the fact that Priscilla wanted to do her own thing," wrote the self-righteous fan. "But she should have done that before she married Elvis. Her life, after her marriage, should have been completely devoted to him, as his wife. Millions of girls and women would have given anything for that chance." No doubt much of Priscilla's mail was considerably more vitriolic. For years she was the victim of death threats, and her popularity after the divorce was virtually nonexistent. A survey of audiences taken in the 1970s showed that the two most disliked people in show business were Howard Cosell and Priscilla Presley. She found herself trapped in a very negative image.

But perhaps the most important reason Priscilla maintained her long silence was her desire to protect Elvis and his memory. She resented the lurid stories that appeared about him, the dime-store psychologizing that dissected his emotional flaws, the accusations that even as a musician he was nothing special. She refused to add any more fuel to the fire. Elvis was, after all, the man she had loved for years ... perhaps still did love even after they were separated by divorce and even death. The least she could do for him now was to protect him.

But by the time of that fiftieth birthday, Priscilla was beginning to come to terms with her memories. And she was also beginning to feel, thanks to her success on *Dallas*, that the public was interested in her for herself, not just because she had once been married to Elvis Presley. For years his shadow had hung over everything she tried to do on her own. She told a British reporter, "I have felt robbed of my own life. Can you imagine what it's like to carry that name? I know that people who look at me see me as a museum piece. They're interested in me as a curiosity, like Elvis's glass-cased guitar or his gold Cadillac." But once audiences began to think of her as the actress who plays Jenna Wade, she felt secure enough about her separate identity to pay public tribute to her own memories of Elvis.

The first indication of this change in her attitude came when she agreed to act as hostess for a filmed tour of Graceland that would be shown as an hour-long special on television the night of his birthday. The director was Steve Binder, who had directed the very successful Christmas special by Elvis that had helped turn his career around. Binder had also directed a later release, *Elvis: One Night With You*, which was composed largely of concert footage Binder had shot for the earlier special but never used. Priscilla knew Steve Binder and felt comfortable with him. So she accepted his offer to act as hostess for the program, and the tour of Graceland, with which she felt such a strong emotional connection.

Binder knew what he wanted the special to be. His first step was to send Priscilla a tape of the tour of the White House conducted in 1963 by a shy but radiant Jackie Kennedy. Binder knew that to rock fans the home of Elvis was just as important as the White House, and he thought the tour could be handled the same way. It gave Priscilla the chance to point out the restoration she had done, bringing Graceland back to the way Elvis had loved it best.

Unquestionably, hosting the show was a difficult experience for Priscilla. Binder said, "While she guarded her feelings pretty well, it was obviously tough on her." People on the set reported that she choked up several times, from the emotions that the house and the script provoked. But she reacted like a pro, pulled herself together, and went on with the work she had to do. It was an important victory for her.

At the time Priscilla told a friend that she hoped that doing the Graceland special would write the final chapter of her life with Elvis and enable her to close the book. But a funny thing happened: Once she revealed a few of her personal memories of Elvis to the public, she realized that she had many more to share. And she also realized that she had a reason to share them.

Her primary motive was the feeling that most of the scores of books written about the life of Elvis Presley were "rumors, misconceptions and lies." Either they were pure adulatory drivel that glossed over any problems in the life of the King, or they were nasty hatchet jobs that showed him at his worst. One of these books came out even before Elvis died. Former employees Red and Sonny West, along with Dave Hebler, wrote *Elvis, What Happened?* which came out in the summer of 1977, just before Elvis died. It revealed for the first time his use of drugs, his love of guns and violence, his thoughtless womanizing; in short, what the cover copy called "The Dark Other Side" of Elvis Presley. Much of this material later found its way into Albert Goldman's bestseller *Elvis*, which also accentuated the negative about the star's life. Priscilla, observing the publication of such books, commented, "It's cruel, and I knew it would happen."

So perhaps it was time to tell the real story of Elvis Presley: to admit the bad but also remember the good. "I feel I owe it to his fans," she explained. "I just want people to know and love him." That included her daughter. Priscilla had been disturbed by the effect of some of the very negative reports about Elvis on Lisa. "One day, when she was just into puberty, an article appeared that depicted her father as a sexual deviate. Lisa came home from school crying, 'One of the kids told me about my dad. Mom, is it true? I would just *hate* him if he was that way!'... It really had a big impact on her at the time, and she went through a period of being angry and disgusted and disliking him. I was very disturbed about it."

Rick Stanley, Elvis's stepbrother, was aware of Lisa's need to come to terms with the reality of her father's life. "I want her to be proud of her father, but to understand that the man was so wrapped up in himself that he couldn't see out the window, that sometimes he wasn't a respecter of persons because he never had to answer to anybody. I want her to understand the position he was in, how hard it is to have anything you want any time you want it and still stay sane."

Priscilla wanted her daughter to understand the truth about her father, too, because she knew that the real truth was more positive than most of the stories that were circulating. She said firmly, "I have beautiful memories—good more than bad." It was finally time to come to terms with those memories and to let the world see the Elvis Presley she had known. Shortly after taping the Graceland special, Priscilla was working

in earnest on a book about her life with Elvis.

That book was published in August, 1985,
and it was an immediate and enormous success with the reading public. *Elvis and Me*
rose to the very top of the best-seller list and
stayed there for weeks. An excerpt appeared
in *People,* and Priscilla was invited on in-
numerable talk shows to discuss the book.
It seemed as if the whole world had been
waiting to hear Priscilla's real feelings about
Elvis. Her continued love and respect for her
former husband shine through nearly every
page. Even when she talks about his problem with drugs, the pain she felt when she
learned about his affairs with other women,
or the loneliness of the last years of their
marriage, her view of Elvis remains tender
and loving. And her book is a welcome antidote to the unpleasant portraits that have
been printed elsewhere. Surely Elvis Presley's faults were enormous...but so were
his gifts. He had a genuinely loving heart
and a generous nature. He could be warm,
funny, charming, and very romantic—just
as his fans had always believed. There was
a child deep within Elvis that never grew
up, and that was the source both of most
of his problems and of his great lovability.
Priscilla had the courage to reveal both aspects of the man she loved.

Writing about Elvis helped Priscilla clarify
her own feelings about the man she had

loved and left. She came to realize that "Elvis carried a heavy burden, tenfold that of any other celebrity. He didn't belong to me, he belonged to the world." Looking back, she also learned more about what love really is. "I realize now more than I did then when I was still so young that you may *think* you know what love is, but you don't know what it really is until you've accumulated all the experiences—all the fights, the words said and unsaid, all the forgiving, all the crying, all the pain."

Priscilla Beaulieu Presley is a woman who has learned the art of survival. So is her daughter. Priscilla is proud of the person her daughter has grown up to be. "Lisa's a very special young lady. She's very reserved, quiet and cautious, like me. But after you get to know her, she's neat." She reflects on her role as a parent: "I guess I'll not know how successful I am as a parent until Lisa is my age and can look back. But right at this moment, I'm just happy that she's happy."

Both mother and daughter have at last managed to find a way to deal with the past. "One thing we have learned is there's just so much suffering you can relive before it destroys you. We try to remember the good times to stay on top of it."

Bibliography

The following materials have been especially helpful to the author in researching the book.

BOOKS

Goldman, Albert. *Elvis.* New York: McGraw-Hill Book Company, 1981.

Harms, Valerie. *Trying to Get to You.* New York: Atheneum, 1979.

Hopkins, Jerry. *Elvis.* New York: Simon & Schuster, 1971.

———. *Elvis: The Final Years.* New York: St. Martin's Press, 1980.

Mann, May: *Elvis and the Colonel.* New York: Drake Publishers, 1975.

———. *Elvis, Why Won't They Leave You Alone?* New York: Signet Books, 1982.

Presley, Dee, with Billy, Rick, and David Stanley, as told to Martin Torgoff. *Elvis, We Love You Tender.* New York: Delacorte Press, 1980.

Presley, Priscilla Beaulieu, with Sandra Harmon. *Elvis and Me.* New York: G.P. Putnam's Sons, 1985.

Van Wormer, Laura. *Dallas.* Garden City, NY: Doubleday & Co, 1985.

West, Red, Sonny West, and Dave Hebler, as told to Steve Dunleavy. *Elvis, What Happened?* New York: Ballantine Books, 1977.

Wootten, Richard. *Elvis!* New York: Random House, 1985.

Yancey, Becky, and Cliff Linedecker. *My Life with Elvis.* New York: St. Martin's Press, 1977.

ARTICLES

Armstrong, Lois. "Priscilla Presley Finds a Vocation—and Michael Landon Some Frustration—On Location", *People*, Nov. 8, 1982.

Battelle, Phyllis. "Priscilla Presley: Her Struggle to Raise Elvis's Daughter," *Ladies' Home Journal*, Feb. 1984.

Fiore, Mary. "Priscilla Presley: Bringing Up Elvis's Daughter," *Ladies' Home Journal*, June 1974.

Kaye, Elizabeth. "Elvis's Other Women," *US*, Oct. 7, 1985.

———. "Life After Elvis," *TV Guide*, Sept. 20, 1980.

O'Hallaren, Bill. "The Ticklish Plight of Being Priscilla Presley," *TV Guide*, March 17, 1984.

People. "Off the Screen: Priscilla Presley," Dec. 4, 1978.

People. "Anniversary: Elvis," Jan. 14, 1985.

Rayl, Shelley. "Did Colonel Parker Take the King for a Ride? A Lawyer for Elvis's Daughter and Sole Heir Says Yes," *People*, Dec. 1, 1980.

Ross, Shelley. "From Elvis to *Dallas*," *McCall's*, Feb. 1984.

Russell, Sue. "'Don't Look Back.' Believes Priscilla Presley, Who's Forging Ahead with a New Career," *US*, Aug. 5, 1980.

Warhol, Andy. "Priscilla Presley," *Interview*, Dec. 1979.

Weller, Sheila. "Priscilla Presley: Surviving Elvis," *McCall's*, May 1979.

Recommended Reading from SIGNET and MENTOR